PASTORAL SPANISH, Volume 1

ISBN 0-88432-689-6 text and cassette
ISBN 1-57970-150-7 text and CDs
ISBN 0-88432-690-X 2- texts

Published by Audio-Forum
One Orchard Park Road
Madison, CT 06405
www.audioforum.com

Acknowledgments

I am grateful for the support and encouragement from my
friends and colleagues at Mount St. Mary College in Newburgh,
New York, especially Sister Ann Sakac, O.P., President, Sister
Agnes Boyle, O.P., Vice President for Academic Affairs, and
Dr. Irene Nunnari and members of the Department of
Communication Arts, Sister Sylvia Bielen, O.P., Professor of
Art, Sister Estelle McKeever, O.P., librarian.

All biblical references are taken from *LA BIBLIA (traducida,
presentada y comentada para las communidades cristiannas
de Latinoamérica y para los que buscan a Dios)*, Ediciones
Paulinas, LXVI edition, Madrid, 1972.

The voice recordings of Volume 1 are by Carolina Castro (El
Salvador) and José Marcos López (México). I wish to also thank
the following students from Mount St. Mary College and
parishioners of St. Patrick's Church, Newburgh, who assisted in
this project: Eileen Blas, Salvador González, Patricia Castro,
Daisy Sánchez, Juana Miranda and Geraldo de Porres.

We acknowledge with thanks the contribution of two other
individuals in the preparation of the text materials: Susan
Rushford, undergraduate alumnus and current graduate
student, who served as consultant and proofreader and John
McCarthy, who gave selflessly his time as computer consultant.

I0170732

INTRODUCTION

Welcome to Volume I of *Pastoral Spanish*. This volume covers basic and intermediate grammar through the use of repetition exercises, substitution drills, dialogs and listening comprehension exercises. Everything contained in Volume I is planned to develop logically useful phrases and sentences. A major portion of the vocabulary in Volume 1 is taken from the homilies in Volume 2. Each chapter review includes material from preceding chapters. Repetition exercises are alternated with substitution drills to allow you to use the new material. Short dialogs and comprehension exercises introduce vocabulary and provide some cultural information.

The longer dialogs in the early chapters are meant to suggest a pattern for realistic conversation as well as a review of grammar and vocabulary of the chapter. Some verb forms introduced in these dialogs are explained in later chapters. Numbers used in the recording refer to grammar or vocabulary and cultural notes. Grammar explanations are kept to a minimum since the immediate goal is conversation and the ability to read aloud. A pronunciation guide and additional exercises are provided in the Appendix.

Repetition is the key to this program aimed at those who work with Latin American parishioners. There has been an effort in Volume 1 to be non-gender exclusive.

We recommend listening to the tapes while following along with the Spanish and English tapescripts the first few times. The response is indicated by italics in the tapescripts. Eventually the student should understand the concepts and be able to respond without the tapescripts.

No professional actors have been used in the recordings. Speakers have been selected based on a standard Latin American accent. The pace of the speakers is normal but at first will seem too fast. As is common in Latin America, the *s* is not always pronounced by the speakers. By hearing a male and a female voice from different countries, you will find it easier to understand and adjust to Spanish-speaking parishioners.

TABLE OF CONTENTS

Introduction and acknowledgements ... i

Chapter 1   BAPTISM   Getting general information for forms; NECESITO and QUISIERA with objects and verbs; TENER with objects and TENER idioms; numbers 1-100; Colors; Agreement of nouns and adjectives; Greetings; Dialog to arrange a baptism; Grammar; Vocabulary and cultural notes ... 1

Chapter 2   "SWEET 15" or LA QUINCEAÑERA   Present tense verbs; Telling time; Setting a date; General office conversation; Introduction to the imperfect tense; Dialog to arrange a *quinceañera*; Grammar; Vocabulary and cultural notes ... 16

Chapter 3   WEDDING   More practice with present and imperfect tense verbs; SABER, CONOCER, CREER, PODER; Verbs that indicate obligation (DEBER, TENER QUE, HAY QUE); Personal "a"; Dialog to arrange a wedding; Grammar; Vocabulary and cultural notes ... 30

Chapter 4   A HAPPY OCCASION: THE NEW YEAR   GUSTARLE with objects and infinitives; Indirect object pronouns with DAR, DECIR, EXPLICAR, ENSEÑAR; IR + A + infinitive and the future tense; Present tense verb drills; Grammar; Vocabulary and cultural notes ... 42

Chapter 5   A SAD OCCASION: SICKNESS AND DEATH   SER with general description, profession and nationality; ESTAR with health and location; SER, ESTAR and TENER compared; Demonstrative adjectives; Unequal comparisons and superlatives; Dialog to arrange a funeral; Grammar; Vocabulary and cultural notes ... 54

Chapter 6   ASH WEDNESDAY AND LENT   The present subjunctive; Commands and the FAVOR DE structure; Subjunctive with indirect commands, wishing, hoping, emotion, doubt and impersonal phrases; Comprehension exercises on Hispanics in the U.S.A.; Grammar; Vocabulary and cultural notes ... 68

Chapter 7   PALM SUNDAY   Present tense review; Preterite tense introduced; Direct object
pronouns; Adverbs; Comprehension exercise on Colombia and the
Galapagos Islands; Grammar; Vocabulary and cultural notes   81

Chapter 8   GOOD FRIDAY   Reflexives; Review of present and future tenses; Cardinal numbers
1-2000; Ordinal numbers; ANTES / DESPUÉS (adverbs and prepositions);
Imperfect and preterite tenses compared; Reflexive and direct object
pronouns used together; Grammar   94

Chapter 9   EASTER   Vocabulary related to Easter; Formation of past participles; Present perfect
and pluperfect tenses; Some questions as preparation for confession;
Uses of the prepositions PARA / POR; Comprehension exercise about
Mount St. Mary Convent; Grammar   105

Chapter 10   CHRISTMAS EVE   Review of the preterite tense; Imperfect subjunctive; Vocabulary
related to Christmas; Conditional tense; Indirect discourse with future and
conditional tense; Contrary to fact phrases; Comprehension exercise
about St. Patrick's Church; Grammar; Vocabulary and cultural notes   116

Chapter 11   CHRISTMAS   Formation of present participles or gerunds; Present and imperfect
progressive tenses; Passive voice; The Christmas Story; Vocabulary building;
Grammar   127

APPENDIX   Guide to Spanish pronunciation; Additional grammar exercises   138

CHAPTER 1

BAPTISM

TAPESCRIPT

(Listen and Repeat)

Necesito	I need
Necesito un libro. (1-A) [See Grammar]	I need a book.
unos libros.	I need some books.
una pluma. (1-a) [See Vocabulary]	a pen.
unas plumas.	some pens.
Necesito el libro.	I need the book.
los libros.	the books.
la pluma.	the pen.
las plumas.	the pens.
Necesito el papel.	I need the paper.
los papeles.	the papers.
Necesito saber.	I need to know.
Necesito hablar.	I need to speak.
Necesito regresar.	I need to return.
Necesito saber	I need to know
su nombre. (1-B)	your name (his, her, your).
el nombre.	the name.
el nombre de usted. (Ud.) (1-C)	your name.
el nombre de la niña. (1-b)	the girl's name (of the girl).
el nombre del niño.	the boy's name (of the boy).
el nombre del padre.	the father's name.
el nombre de la madre.	the mother's name.
el nombre de soltera de la madre.	the mother's maiden name.

Quisiera saber   (1-c)

I should or would like to know

su dirección. — your address (his, her, their).
la dirección. — the address.
las direcciones. — the addresses.
la calle. — the street.
el número. — the number.
el número de la calle. — the number of the street.
el apartamento. — the apartment.
el número del apartamento. — the number of the apartment.
la ciudad. — the city.

Tengo el nombre del pueblo. — I have the name of the town.
Tengo un apartamento. — I have an apartment.
Tengo unas plumas. — I have some pens.
Tengo unos datos personales. — I have some personal information.
Tengo una casa. — I have a house.

Tengo el teléfono. — I have the phone.
NO tengo el teléfono. (1-D) — I don't have the phone.
el número de teléfono — the phone number
No tengo el número de teléfono. — I don't have the phone number.

¿Tiene usted (Ud.)? (1-E) — Do you have?
¿Tiene usted (Ud.) los papeles? — Do you have the papers?
--Sí, tengo los papeles. — Yes, I have the papers.
--No, no tengo los papeles. — No, I don't have the papers.
¿Tiene usted (Ud.) la dirección? — Do you have the address?
--Sí, tengo la dirección. — Yes, I have the address.
--No, no tengo la dirección. — No, I don't have the address.

el padre — the father
la madre — the mother
los padres — the parents (or the fathers)
el padrino — the godfather
la madrina — the godmother
los padrinos — the godparents (or godfathers)
católico (1-d) — Catholic (adjective)
el católico — the Catholic man
católica — Catholic (feminine adjective)
la católica — the Catholic woman

¿ Es católico el padrino?
¿ Es católica la madrina?

Is the godfather Catholic?
Is the godmother Catholic?

LOS NÚMEROS

NUMBERS

Uno....dos....tres....cuatro....cinco...
seis.....siete.....ocho....nueve....diez
siete sacramentos   diez plumas
once....doce....trece....catorce....quince
dieciséis....diecisiete...dieciocho...diecinueve
veinte....veintiuno....veintidós....veintitrés...veinticuatro
veinticinco....veintiséis....veintisiete...veintiocho
veintinueve...treinta...treinta y uno.....treinta y dos
cuarenta....cuarenta y tres....cuarenta y cinco
cincuenta...cincuenta y cinco....cincuenta y ocho

1...2...3...4...5...
6.....7.....8......9....10
7 sacraments 10 pens
11...12....13....14....15
16...17...18...19...
20...21...22....23...24
25...26....27...28
29....30....31....32
40....43....45
50...55....58

¿ CUÁNTOS? (1-E)

HOW MANY? (HOW MUCH?)

¿Cuántos libros?
¿Cuántos libros tiene usted (Ud.)?
(cinco)--Tengo cinco libros.
(veinte)--Tengo veinte libros.
¿ Cuántos libros tiene el señor? (doce) (1-F)
--El señor tiene doce libros.
¿ Cuántos libros tiene la señora? (trece)
--La señora tiene trece libros.
¿ CUÁNTAS plumas tiene ella ? (venticuatro)
--Ella tiene veinticuatro plumas.
¿Cuántas hermanas tiene José? (tres)
--José tiene tres hermanas.

How many books?
How many books do you have?
(5) I have five books.
(20) I have 20 books.
How many books does the man have? (12)
The man has 12 books.
How many books does the woman have? (13)
The woman has 13 books.
How many pens does she have? (24)
She has 24 pens.
How many sisters does Joseph have? (3)
Joseph has 3 sisters.

¿Cuántos libros HAY?   (1-G)
--Hay un libro.
--Hay dos libros.
--Hay muchos libros.
los meses
¿Cuántos meses HAY en un año? (doce)
--HAY doce meses.

How many books are there?
There is one book.
There are two books.
There are many books.
the months
How many months are there in a year? (12)
There are 12 months.

LOS MESES DEL AÑO	THE MONTHS OF THE YEAR
enero....febrero....marzo.....abril mayo.....junio....julio....agosto septiembre...octubre...noviembre...diciembre	January....February...March....April May .....June....July.....August September..October...November..December
Primero de enero, dos de febrero, tres de marzo, cuatro de abril, cinco de mayo, seis de junio, siete de julio, San Fermín	January 1st, February 2, March 3, April 4, May 5, June 6 July 7, day of St. Fermin (from a Spanish folksong) (St. Fermin is the patron saint of bullfighters)
Hoy es el ocho de marzo. Mañana es el nueve de marzo. el día---los días Hay siete días en una semana. Los días de la semana son... lunes...martes....miércoles...jueves (1-H) viernes...sábado...domingo el fin de semana El fin de semana es sábado y domingo. Hoy es lunes. Mañana es martes. la fecha ¿Cuál es la fecha de hoy? --Hoy es jueves el cinco de enero. (1-I) --Hoy es el quince de octubre. ¿CUÁNDO? nacimiento fecha de nacimiento ¿Cuándo es su fecha de nacimiento?	Today is March 8. Tomorrow is March 9. the day---the days There are 7 days in a week. The days of the week are... Monday...Tuesday...Wednesday...Thursday Friday...Saturday...Sunday the weekend The weekend is Saturday and Sunday. Today is Monday. Tomorrow is Tuesday. the date What is today's date? Today is Thursday, January 5. Today is October 15. When? birth date of birth When is your (his, her, their) date of birth?

Necesito saber
    la fecha de nacimiento.
    el lugar.
    el lugar de nacimiento.
	I need to know
	    the date of birth.
	    the place.
	    the place of birth.

bautismo
primera comunión
la boda
¿Cuándo es la fecha del bautismo?
¿Cuándo es la fecha de la primera comunión?
Necesito saber la fecha del bautismo.
Quisiera saber la fecha del bautismo.

baptism
first communion
the wedding
When is the date of the baptism?
When is the date of the first communion?
I need to know the date of the baptism.
I would like to know the date of the baptism.

¿CUÁNTOS AÑOS TIENE la niña (el niño)? (1-e)
¿Qué edad tiene la niña (el niño)?
--Ella (él) tiene ocho años.
--Ella tiene ocho meses.
--Ella tiene tres días.
¿Cuántos años tiene usted (Ud.)?
--Tengo cuarenta y ocho años.
¿Qué edad tiene usted (Ud.)?
--Tengo veintitrés años.

How old is the girl (boy)?
What is the age of the girl (boy)?
She (he) is 8 years old.
She is 8 months old.
She is 3 days old.
How old are you?
I am 48 years old.
What's your age?
I am 23 years old.

MÁS NÚMEROS

MORE NUMBERS

diez........veinte....treinta......cuarenta....cincuenta
sesenta...sesenta y uno....sesenta y dos
setenta... ochenta...noventa...cien
ciento uno...ciento dos...ciento tres...ciento cuatro
ciento quince...ciento dieciséis...doscientos

10...20...30...40...50
60...61...62
70...80...90...100
101...102...103...104
115...116...200

FILLING OUT FORMS: PRACTICAL PHRASES, QUESTIONS AND ANSWERS

Necesito saber su nombre.
Quisiera saber su nombre.
¿Cómo se llama Ud?
--Me llamo José Sánchez . (1-f)
--Me llamo Ana Gómez Flores.
--Mi nombre es Carlos Pérez.

I need to know your name.
I would like to know your name.
What is your name?
My name is Jose Sanchez.
My name is Ana Gómez Flores.
My name is Carlos Perez.

¿Cómo se llama la niña (el niño)?
--La niña (el niño) se llama _____

What is the girl's (boy's) name?
The girl's (boy's) name is _____

Necesito saber su dirección.	I need to know your address.
¿Dónde vive Ud?	Where do you live?
--Vivo en la calle Washington, 35.	I live at 35 Washington Street.
--Vivo en Brooklyn.	I live in Brooklyn.
--Mi dirección es la avenida Main, apartamento 3-A en Chicago.	My address is apt. 3-A Main Ave. in Chicago.
Necesito saber su número de teléfono.	I need to know your phone number.
¿Cuál es su número de teléfono?	What is your phone number?
--Mi teléfono es el tres-cuatro-cinco-seis- dos- ocho-nueve.	My phone number is 345-6289.
Necesito la fecha de nacimiento del niño.	I need the boy's (child's) date of birth.
¿CUÁNDO nació el niño?	When was the child born?
--El niño nació el tres de febrero.	The child was born February 3.
mil novecientos...	19---
mil novecientos ochenta y siete	1987
mil novecientos noventa y uno	1991
Necesito saber el lugar de nacimiento.	I need to know the place of birth.
¿DÓNDE nació el niño?	Where was the boy born?
--El niño nació en Austin, Texas.	The boy was born in Austin, Texas.
¿Cuándo nació usted (Ud.)?	When were you born?
--Nací el dos de abril de mil novecientos cuarenta y dos.	I was born on April 2, 1942.
--Nací el veinticinco de mayo de mil novecientos sesenta.	I was born on May 25, 1960.
--Nací el quince de enero de mil novecientos treinta y tres.	I was born on January 15, 1933.
¿Dónde nació usted (Ud.)?	Where were you born?
--Nací en Santiago de Cuba.	I was born in Santiago, Cuba.
--Nací en Puerto Rico.	I was born in Puerto Rico.

REVIEW OF NOUN--ADJECTIVE AGREEMENT

(Listen and Repeat)

El hijo es sincero.	The son is sincere.
El hijo es amable.	The son is nice (kind).
La hija es sincera.	The daughter is sincere.

El vestido es blanco.
La iglesia es pequeña.
El hermano es grande.
El padrino es católico.
La madrina es católica.
(un hombre) Ud. es católico. // Soy católico.
(una mujer) Ud. es católica. // Soy católica.
Es una costumbre judía.
Es un libro judío.
Es una tradición protestante.

The dress is white.
The church is small.
The brother is big.
The godfather is Catholic.
The godmother is Catholic.
(a man) You are Catholic // I am Catholic.
(a woman) You are Catholic // I am Catholic.
It is a Jewish custom.
It is a Jewish book.
It is a Protestant tradition.

UNOS COLORES

blanco
negro
rojo
verde
azul
amarillo
color café
morado

SOME COLORS

white
black
red
green
blue
yellow
brown (coffee color)
purple

El vestido es blanco.
El vestido es azul.
La luz es verde.
La luz es amarilla.

The dress is white.
The dress is blue.
The light is green.
The light is yellow.

(Repeat the following sentences first in the singular, then in the plural)

La iglesia es grande.---Las iglesias son grandes.
Mi casa es nueva.---Mis casas son nuevas.
Mi hermano es pequeño.---Mis hermanos son pequeños.
El sacramento es especial.---Los sacramentos son especiales.
La vela es blanca.---Las velas son blancas.
Su regalo es bonito.---Sus regalos son bonitos.
Nuestro documento es importante.---Nuestros documentos
    son importantes.

The church is big.---The churches are big.
My house is new.---My houses are new.
My brother is small.---My brothers are small.
The sacrament is special.---The sacraments are special.
The candle is white.---The candles are white.
Your (his, her) gift is pretty. ---Your gifts are pretty.
Our document is important.---Our documents
are important.

NOUN-ADJECTIVE WORD ORDER   (Repetition)

su vestido blanco	her (your) white dress
nuestras velas blancas	our white candles
mis hermanas grandes	my big sisters
mi hermano pequeño	my little brother
los esposos católicos	the Catholic husband and wife (spouses)
Nuestra Señora de Guadalupe	Our Lady of Guadalupe
un problema difícil	a difficult problem
unas costumbres judías	some Jewish customs
los padres cariñosos	the affectionate parents

El vestido blanco del bautismo es símbolo
   de la gracia y de la inocencia.

The white dress of baptism is a symbol
   of grace and innocence.

UNOS SALUDOS

SOME GREETINGS

Hola	Hello
Buenos días	Good morning
Buenas tardes	Good afternoon
Buenas noches	Good evening (good night)
¿Cómo está Ud?	How are you?
--Bien, gracias, ¿y Ud?	Fine, and you?
¿Cómo está la familia?	How is your family?
¿Qué hay de nuevo?	What's new?
--Nada. Todo va bien.	Nothing. Everything is fine.
Le presento a-------	Let me introduce you to----
Mucho gusto.	Nice to meet you.
Adiós. Hasta luego. Hasta la vista.	Good bye . See you soon.
¡Felicitaciones! (¡enhorabuena!)	Congratulations!
¡Felicito a Ud! (a ustedes)	I congratulate you (all)
Le deseo muchas felicidades.	I wish you much happiness.
Gracias.	Thanks.
Gracias por el regalo.	Thanks for the gift.

BREVE DIÁLOGO PARA ARREGLAR UN BAUTISMO

(El sacerdote conversa con una feligresa.)

SEÑORA--Buenos días, padrecito.(1-g) Quisiera el bautismo de mi hijito lo más pronto posible. Mis padres están aquí de visita y pronto necesitan regresar a México.

PADRE--Muy bien, señora Rodríguez. Necesito saber unos datos personales. ¿Cómo se llama su hijo?

SEÑORA--Mi hijito se llama Carlos Rodríguez García. Como Ud. sabe, me llamo Isabel García de Rodríguez y mi esposo es Tomás Rodríguez Sánchez.

PADRE--Bueno. Necesito su dirección.

SEÑORA--Vivimos en la Avenida Troy, 38, apartamento 9-A.

PADRE-- ¿Dónde se casaron Uds.?

SEÑORA--Nos casamos en la Iglesia de Santa Rosa en Puebla, México.

PADRE-- ¿Cuándo y dónde nació su hijo Carlos?

SEÑORA--Carlos nació el 3 de febrero de 1991 en Nueva York.

PADRE--Necesito saber su número de teléfono.

SEÑORA--Nuestro teléfono es el 861-3442.

PADRE--Excelente. ¿Cómo se llaman los padrinos? Comprenden ellos la importancia del bautismo? ¿Son católicos los padrinos? Necesito hablar con con todos ustedes antes del bautismo.

SEÑORA--Muy bien. Hoy es una charla (plática) preliminar. El padrino se llama Diego Ojeda y la madrina es su esposa,

BRIEF DIALOG TO ARRANGE A BAPTISM

(The priest converses with a female parishioner.)

Good morning, Father. I would like the baptism of my little son as soon as possible. My parents are visiting and soon need to return to Mexico.

Very good, Mrs. Rodriguez. I need to know some personal information. What is your son's name?

My son is named Carlos Rodriguez Garcia. As you know, my name is Isabel García de Rodriguez and my husband is Tomas Rodriguez Sanchez.

Good. I need your address.

We live at 38 Troy Ave., Apt 9-A.

Where were you married?

We got married in the Church of St. Rose in Puebla, Mexico.

When and where was your son born?

Carlos was born on February 3, 1991 in New York.

I need to know your phone number.

Our phone is 861-3442.

Excellent. What are the names of the godparents? Do they understand the importance of baptism? Are the godparents Catholic? I need to speak to all of you before the baptism.

Very good. Today is a preliminary talk. The godfather's name is Diego Ojeda and the godmother is his wife, Carolina.

Carolina Espinosa. Son católicos. ¿Podemos hablar el jueves cuando no trabajan nuestros esposos y tener el bautismo el sábado?

Can we talk on Thursday when our husbands aren't working and have the baptism on Saturday?

PADRE--Necesito ver el horario. El jueves a las cinco está bien para la plática. Tengo los bautismos los sábados a las diez y media. Es importante ser puntual. El niño necesita un vestido blanco para la ceremonia. Hasta el jueves.

I need to see the schedule. Thursday at 5:00 is good. I have baptisms on Saturdays at 10:30. It is important to be punctual. The child needs a white dress (garment) for the ceremony. Until Thursday.

SEÑORA--Gracias, padrecito. Hasta luego.

Thank you, Father. Until we meet again.

PADRE--De nada. Hasta luego.

You are welcome. Until we meet again.

GRAMMAR

1-A GENDER AGREEMENT, SINGULAR AND PLURAL

As in other Romance languages, Spanish has masculine or feminine words. **Nouns and adjectives must agree in gender and number** (singular and plural).

    masculine singular: **el libro** (the book) **un** libro (a book)
    masculine plural: **los libros** (the books) **unos** libros (some books)

    feminine singular: **la pluma** (the pen) **una** pluma (a pen)
    feminine plural: **las** plumas (the pens) **unas** plumas (some pens)

A word ending in -E of either gender can be made plural by simply adding -S
    una calle (a street)   unas calles (some streets)   un nombre (a name)   unos nombres (some names)

Words that do not end in a vowel add -ES for the plural form.
    el papel (the paper)   un papel (a paper)   los papeles (the papers)   unos papeles (some papers)
    la ciudad (the city)   una ciudad (a city)   las ciudades (the cities)   unas ciudades (some cities)

Words that end in -Z drop the last letter and add -CES for the plural: La luz--las luces (light); el lápiz--los lápices (pencil).

A few words end in -A but are masculine: el día (the day) ; el problema (the problem); el dilema (the dilemma); el idioma; (the language); el mapa (the map); el profeta (prophet). Sometimes, though rarely, gender will change the meaning on a word:

el cura (the priest)   la cura (the cure)   el radio (the radius)   la radio (the radio)

Agreement by gender and number must be kept in the entire phrase. Note that the word order of noun and adjective is usually reversed between English and Spanish. Dictionaries give all adjectives in the masculine singular form.

la   niña   generosa
the   girl   generous [literal]   (the generous girl)

los   papeles blancos
the   papers   white [literal]   (the white papers)

la madre cariñosa   (the affectionate mother)
el padre cariñóso   (the affectionate father)

Usted (abbreviated as Ud.), meaning *you* can be masculine or feminine by meaning.
Usted es sincero. (You are sincere.) [a man]   Usted es sincera. (You are sincere.) [a woman]

Yo meaning *I* is similar. Yo soy sincero. (I am sincere.) [man speaking]
Yo soy sincera. (I am sincere.) [woman speaking]

Adjectives that do not end in -O or -A only change for plurals.
Ud. es amable. (You are nice.) [man or woman]
Yo soy inteligente. (I am intelligent.) [man or woman]
Ud. es especial.-- Yo soy especial. (You are special.--I am special.) [man or woman]

1-B POSSESSIVE ADJECTIVES

Possessive adjectives (my, his, your) always are placed before the noun, as in English.
MI libro (my book)   SU libro (his, her, your or their book)

Generally agreement is only by singular or plural, not gender.
MIS libros (my books)   SUS libros (his, her, your or their book)

NUESTRO/A (our) is the only possessive adjective that agrees also by gender.
nuestro libro (our book)   nuestros libros (our books)
nuestra calle (our street)   nuestras calles (our streets)

SU---SUS can mean *his, her, your* or *their*. Usually the meaning is clear.
        Usted tiene su libro.   (You have your book.)
        Ella tiene su libro.   (She has her book.)
        Carlos tiene sus libros. (Carlos has his books.)
        Ellos tienen su libro.   (They have their book.)
        Usted tiene sus libros. (You have your books.)

If the meaning of SU or SUS is unclear, a phrase can be added for clarification.

    su nombre or el nombre de usted (your name)
                el nombre de ella   (her name)
                el nombre de él   (his name)
                el nombre de ellos (their name)

1-C ABBREVIATIONS are few but they are always capitalized in Spanish.

    Ud. [usted] (you)   Uds. [ustedes] (you -plural)
    Sr. [señor] (Mr.)   Sra. [señora] (Mrs.)   Srita./ Srta. [señorita] (Miss)
    Dr. [doctor] (Dr.)   Dra. [doctora] (Dr. -feminine)
    Fr. [fray] (religious brother or priest) Fr. Javier--used with first names
    D. or don (formally used with nobility) don Bernardo--used with first name and is used sometimes for priests.
    Hna. [hermana] (religious sister) (Hna. Silvia) Sor, also used with the first name of a nun, is not abbreviated.

1-D MAKING SENTENCES NEGATIVE in Spanish only requires the word *no* before the verb .

    El libro es grande   (The book is big.)
    El libro no es grande. (The book is not big.)

1-E FORMING QUESTIONS

The usual word order for a statement in Spanish is subject before verb, as in English.
    Ella tiene el libro.   El padrino es católico.
    (She has the book.)   (The godfather is Catholic.)

The most common way to make a question is to REVERSE THE WORD ORDER to verb before subject and use question marks at both ends of the question.

¿Tiene ella el libro?   ¿Es católico el padrino?
(Does she have the book?)   (Is the godfather Catholic?)

Another way to form a question is to make a statement and ADD A TAG LINE, *¿ no es verdad?* or *¿no?*

Ud. tiene el libro, ¿no es verdad?   (You have the book, isn't that so?)
Ud. tiene el libro, ¿no?   (You have the book, haven't you?)

One can also use INTERROGATIVE WORDS (who, what, where) in questions. All interrogative words in Spanish have an accent.

¿CÓMO? (how?)   ¿Cómo se llama Ud? (literally, How do you call yourself?)
¿CUÁNTO-a-os? (how much, how many?) ¿Cuántos libros tiene Ud.? (How many books do you have?)
¿CUÁNDO? (when?)   ¿Cuándo es el bautismo? (When is the baptism?)
¿CUÁL? (what, which)   ¿Cuál es la fecha? (What is the date?)
¿QUÉ? (what?)   ¿Qué edad tiene Ud? (What is your age?)
¿DÓNDE? (where?)   ¿Dónde nació Ud? (Where were you born?)

In later chapters more interrogative words are introduced.

¿POR QUÉ? (why?)   (porque= because)
¿QUIÉN? (who) ¿para quién? (for whom?)   ¿de quién? (whose?) ¿con quién? (with whom?)

1-F Numbers are spelled out for practice purposes in the exercises. Except for one and hundreds, they do not agree with gender.
un libro (a book or one book)   una madre (a mother or one mother)
cinco libros (five books)   quince calles (fifteen streets)

1-G   HAY = there is // there are
Hay una casa. (There is a house)   Hay 12 meses en un año. (There are 12 months in a year.)

1-H CAPITALIZATION

Spanish grammar books only capitalize the first word in a sentence, proper names, places on maps, abbreviations and references to God, (el Señor-the Lord, su Hijo-His Son). Names of religions, nationalities, languages, days of the week and months are not capitalized. However, many Spanish-speakers capitalize months and sometimes days of the week.

1-I DATES   Again the order is different between English and Spanish.

> January 5   May 15
> 5 de enero   15 de mayo

This is especially important on records for date of birth. January 5, 1972 (1/5/72) = 5 de enero de 1972 (5/1/72)

The first day of the month is the only one that uses the ordinal number: 1 de febrero (primero de febrero).

VOCABULARY AND CULTURAL NOTES

a) *pluma*= pen or feather. Other words for pen are : *el lapicero, el bolígrafo*. In some countries *pluma* now means *fountain pen*.

b) *niño, niño*= girl, boy (child)   There are many words in Spanish used for babies. Some examples are: *nena, nene, criatura, bebé*..

c) *quisiera* (I should like or I would like) This form of the verb QUERER (to want), the imperfect subjunctive, is explained in Chapter 10.   Because it is so useful, it is introduced here. It is more polite than other forms of QUERER (*yo quiero, Ud. quiere*) introduced in Chapter 2. *Quisiera* is especially easy to use because, since it is imperfect subjunctive, it is the same form for first and third person singular: *yo quisiera* (I should /would like)   *Ud., él, ella quisiera* (you, he, she should/would like).

d) Many words in Spanish function as nouns or adjectives, converting easily between masculine and feminine.
   una oración católica--adjective--(a Catholic prayer)
   la católica--noun-- (the Catholic woman)
   el católico--noun-- (the Catholic man)
   los católicos--noun--(the Catholics--men or men and women)
   las católicas--noun--(the Catholics--women only)

Many words referring to family relationships are masculine or feminine: el hijo (son)   la hija (daughter)
                                                                         el hermano (brother) la hermana (sister)

e) Idioms are phrases that do not translate literally between languages. *Tengo*= I have but when used with these phrases means *is:*
   Tengo 24 años.   (I am 24 years old.)   La niña tiene sed.   (The girl is thirsty.)

Other idioms with **TENER** are:

Tengo frío. (I am cold)   Tengo calor. (I am hot)   Tengo hambre. (I am hungry)
Tengo miedo. (I am afraid)   Tengo suerte. (I am lucky)   Tengo sed (I am thirsty)
Tengo prisa. (I am in a hurry.) Tengo razón. (I am right.)   Tengo éxito. (I am successful.)
Tengo sueño. (I am sleepy.)
Tengo que... (I have to or must + a verb in the infinitive)
Tengo que saber su dirección. (I have to know your address.)

More examples of these idiomatic phrases are found in Chapters 3 and 5.

f) It is traditional in most Spanish-speaking countries to use two surnames (*apellidos*), especially on documents. The first last name is the father's and is the more important. The second last name is the mother's.

Ana Gómez Flores = Srita. Gómez   Carlos González Pérez= Sr. González

If these two are married and have a child, he could be called **Carlos González Gómez** . (There is no need for *jr*. in Spanish.) Some women always sign with their maiden names, even if married. Other women drop their mother's name and add *de* and the husband's first last name: Ana Gómez *de* González, meaning *wife of González*. If Hispanic women have lived for some years in in the United States, they may choose to follow the customs here.

g) Diminutives are quite common, especially in Mexico and when referring to children. Diminutives are formed by adding-ITO/-ITA or -ILLO/-ILLA to a word. *Hijito* = my little son is a typical example. The diminutive form for the priest, *padrecito*, shows affection, not disrespect from this Mexican parishioner.

15

CHAPTER 2

"SWEET 15" or *LA QUINCEAÑERA*

TAPESCRIPT

PRESENT TENSE VERBS

(Listen and repeat)

NECESITO unas velas.
   las flores blancas.
   un apartamento.
   un ensayo.
Carlos NECESITA el libro. (2-A)
Marta NECESITA el número.
Ud. (usted) NECESITA los documentos.
Ellos NECESITAN
Uds. (ustedes) NECESITAN
Carlos y Marta necesitan
Ellos necesitan su familia.
Las hijas necesitan un lápiz.
Nosotros NECESITAMOS
Carlos y yo necesitamos
Necesitamos trabajo.
   un apartamento nuevo.
   una fiesta.
Necesito firmar el documento.
Carlos necesita saber la verdad.
Ellos necesitan trabajar.
Necesitamos escribir la carta.

I need some candles.
   the white flowers.
   an apartment.
   a rehearsal.
Carlos needs the book.
Marta needs the number.
You need the documents.
They need
You (pl.) need
Carlos and Marta need
They need their family.
The daughters need a pencil.
We need
Carlos and I need
We need work.
   a new apartment.
   a party.
I need to sign the document.
Carlos needs to know the truth.
They need to work.
We need to write the letter.

TENER
TENGO una sorpresa.
No tengo muchos hermanos.
José TIENE cinco hijos.
Mi hermanito tiene tres años.
Ellos TIENEN
Ellos tienen una casa vieja.
Uds. no tienen un coche.
Los señores García tienen un perro.
Mis padres no tienen un perro.
Los padrinos tienen un regalo.
Nosotros TENEMOS
Tenemos nuestros libros.
Tenemos nuestras velitas.

SER
El padrino ES católico.
Mi abuela es cristiana.
La mujer es cariñosa.
Ud. ES amable.
Ud. es muy amable.
Ellos SON
Nuestros amigos son judíos.
Paco y ella son hermanos, ¿no es verdad? (1-E)
Nuestros amigos son protestantes, ¿no?
Las tradiciones de nuestra iglesia son bonitas.
Yo SOY
Soy un hijo fiel.
Soy católica.
Soy católico.
Soy el abuelo de Anita.
Nosotros SOMOS
Somos hermanos.
Somos esposos y padres.
Todos somos los hijos de Dios.
Somos cristianos.
Él y yo somos hermanos.

TO HAVE
I have a surprise.
I don't have many brothers (and sisters).
Jose has five children.
My little brother is three years old.
They have
They have an old house.
You (pl.) don't have a car.
Mr. and Mrs. Garcia have a dog.
My parents don't have a dog.
The godparents have a gift.
We have
We have our friends.
We have our little candles.

TO BE
The godfather is Catholic.
My grandmother is Christian.
The woman is affectionate.
You are kind.
You are very kind.
They are
Our friends are Jewish.
Paco and she are siblings, isn't that true?
Our friends are Protestant, aren't they?
The traditions of our church are lovely.
I am
I am a faithful son.
I am (a) Catholic (woman).
I am (a) Catholic (man).
I am Anita's grandfather.
We are
We are siblings (brothers, brothers and sisters).
We are spouses (husband-wife) and parents.
We all are the children of God.
We are Christians.
He and I are brothers.(siblings)

LA FAMILIA (repetición)	THE FAMILY
el padre---la madre---los padres	the father---the mother---the parents
el esposo---la esposa---los esposos	the husband---the wife---the spouses
el hijo---la hija---los hijos	the son---the daughter---the children
el tío---la tía	the uncle---the aunt
el primo---la prima	the male cousin---the female cousin
el abuelo---la abuela	the grandfather---the grandmother
el nieto---la nieta	the grandson---the granddaughter
el hermano---la hermana---los hermanos	the brother---the sister---siblings (brothers and sisters)
sobrino---sobrina	the nephew---the niece
El padre de mi madre es mi abuelo.	The father of my mother is my grandfather.
La hija de mi tío es mi prima.	The daughter of my uncle is my cousin.
Los hijos de mi hermano son mis sobrinos.	The children of my brother are my nephew and nieces.
Soy la sobrina de mis tíos.	I am the niece of my uncle and aunt.

Los verbos QUERER y PREFERIR (repetición)	The verbs TO WANT and TO PREFER
¿Qué QUIERE Ud?	What do you want?
--QUIERO un café.	I want some coffee.
--Quiero un refresco.	I want a soft drink.
·Quiero algo.	I want something.
--NO quiero NADA. (2-B)	I don't want anything.

(Substitute with the new noun. The correct answer will follow the pause.)

Quiero un libro. (el correo)	I want a book. (the mail)
Quiero el correo. (unas cartas)	*I want the mail.* (some letters)
Quiero unas cartas. (un papel)	*I want some letters.* (a paper)
Quiero un papel. (algo)	*I want a paper.* (something)
Quiero algo. (no....nada)	*I want something.* (no...nothing)
No quiero nada. (Coca Cola)	*I don't want anything.* (Coca Cola)
No quiero Coca Cola.	*I don't want Coca Cola.*
Siempre quiero Coca Cola.	I always want Coca Cola.
NUNCA quiero Coca Cola. (2-B)	I never want Coca Cola.
NO quiero Coca Cola NUNCA.	I never want Coca Cola.
NO quiero NADA NUNCA.	I never want anything.

(Listen and repeat)

Anita quiere una sorpresa.
Ud. no quiere nada.
El niño siempre quiere chocolates.
Mi nieta quiere una cruz.
Nuestro sacerdote nunca quiere unas vacaciones.

¿Qué quiere Anita? Anita quiere...
¿Qué quiere Ud?   (yo) QUIERO...

¿Qué PREFIERE Ud?
(yo) PREFIERO...
--Prefiero café.
--Prefiero un refresco.

Anita wants a surprise.
You don't want anything.
The child always wants chocolates.
My granddaughter wants a cross.
Our priest never wants a vacation.

What does Anita want? Anita wants...
What do you want? I want...

What do you prefer?
I prefer...
I prefer coffee.
I prefer a soft drink.

(Answer the question with the given answer. The correct answer will follow the pause.)

¿Qué prefiere Ud., café o té? (café)
--*Prefiero café.*
¿Qué prefiere Ud., vino o cerveza? (cerveza)
--*Prefiero cerveza.*
¿Qué prefiere Ud., las vacaciones o el trabajo? (el trabajo)
--*Prefiero el trabajo.*
¿Qué quiere Ud.? (helado)
--*Quiero helado.*
¿Prefiere Ud. chocolate o vainilla? (vainilla)
--*Prefiero vainilla.*

Do you prefer coffee or tea? (coffee)
I prefer coffee.
Do you prefer wine or beer? (beer)
I prefer beer.
Do you prefer a vacation or work? (work)
I prefer work.
What do you want? (ice cream)
I want ice cream.
Do you prefer chocolate or vanilla?
I prefer vanilla.

(Listen and repeat)

Quiero trabajar.--- Prefiero trabajar.
Quiero beber café. --- Prefiero beber café.
José quiere leer. --- José prefiere leer.
Ud. quiere comprar. ---Ud prefiere comprar.
Ellos quieren salir.---Ellos prefieren salir.
Uds. quieren firmar.---Uds. prefieren firmar.
Queremos comer.---Preferimos comer.
Queremos hablar.-- Preferimos hablar.

I want to work. --- I prefer to work.
I want to drink coffee.--- I prefer to drink coffee.
Jose wants to read. --- Jose prefers to read.
You want to buy.---You prefer to buy.
They want to leave.---They prefer to leave.
You (pl.) want to sign.---You prefer to sign.
We want to eat.---We prefer to eat.
We want to talk. --- We prefer to talk.

¿Qué quieren hacer Uds?	What do you want to do?
--Queremos descansar.	We want to rest.
--Queremos hablar por teléfono.	We want to talk on the phone.

LA HORA (2-C) — TELLING TIME

¿Qué hora es?	What time is it?
Es la una.	It is 1:00.
Son las dos.	It is 2:00.
Son las tres y diez.	It is 3:10.
Son las cuatro y quince.	It is 4:15.
Son las cinco y cuarto.	It is 5:15.
¿Qué hora es?	What time is it?
Son las cinco y media.	It is 5:30.
Son las seis menos cuarto (quince).	It is 5:45.
Son las cinco y cuarenta y cinco.	It is 5:45.
Son las siete menos diez.	It is 6:50.
¿Cuándo tienen misa?	When do they have Mass?
--Tienen (hay) misa todos los días a las ocho.	They have (there is) Mass everyday at 8:00.
--Tienen misa los domingos a las siete.	They have mass on Sundays at 7:00.
a las nueve de la mañana	at 9:00 in the morning
a las tres de la tarde	at 3:00 in the afternoon
a las diez y media de la noche	at 10:30 in the evening
muy temprano (muy tarde)	very early (very late)
¿A qué hora...	(at) what time...
¿A qué hora quiere Ud. la quinceañera?	What time do you want the *sweet 15* celebration?
--Quiero la fiesta a las tres.	I want the party at 3:00.
¿A qué hora es la cita ?	What time is the appointment (date) ?
--La cita es a las once y cuarto.	The appointment is at 11:15.
el cumpleaños	the birthday
Quieren una fiesta de cumpleaños.	They want a birthday party.
Quisiera la fiesta el domingo.	I (he or she) would like the party on Sunday.
el domingo que viene.	next Sunday.
el próximo domingo.	next Sunday.
el 3 de mayo a las tres.	on May 3 at 3:00.

SOME PRESENT AND IMPERFECT TENSE VERBS COMPARED (Listen and repeat)

(yo) necesito.......(yo) NECESITABA (2-D)	I need.......I used to need (I needed)

Ahora necesito...Antes necesitaba
Ahora necesito flores...Antes necesitaba flores
(yo) llevo....(yo) LLEVABA
Ahora llevo a mi hija.
Antes llevaba a mi hija.
(yo) trabajo....TRABAJABA
Ahora trabajo en la oficina.
Antes trabajaba en la oficina.

Carlos necesita...Carlos NECESITABA
Ahora Carlos necesita la verdad.
Antes Carlos necesitaba la verdad.
Ahora Carlos lleva...Antes Carlos LLEVABA
Ahora Ud. lleva...Antes Ud. llevaba
Ahora Carlos trabaja...Antes Carlos TRABAJABA
Ahora Ud. trabaja...Antes Ud. trabajaba

Ahora (yo) SOY
Antes (yo) ERA
Ahora soy adulto...Antes era niño.
Ahora Ud. ES adulto...Antes Ud. ERA niño.
Ahora ella es adulta...Antes ella era niña.

Ahora hay un problema...Antes HABÍA un problema.
Ahora hay libros...Antes no había libros.

Ahora tengo...Antes TENÍA
Ahora tengo la sorpresa.
Antes no tenía la sorpresa.
Ahora Carlos tiene
Antes Carlos TENÍA
Ahora Pedro tiene la sorpresa.
Antes Pedro no tenía la sorpresa.
Ahora Ud. tiene el problema.
Antes Ud. no tenía el problema.

Ahora (yo) quiero...Antes (yo) QUERÍA
Ahora quiero leer.
Antes quería leer.

Now I need...Before I used to need
Now I need flowers...Before I used to need flowers
I carry....I used to carry
Now I carry my daughter.
Before I used to carry my daughter.
I work...I used to work
Now I work in the office.
Before I used to work in the office.

Carlos needs...Carlos used to need
Now Carlos needs the truth.
Before Carlos needed the truth.
Now Carlos carries...Before he used to carry
Now you carry...Before you used to carry
Now Carlos works...Before Carlos used to work
Now you work...Before you used to work

Now I am
Before I used to be (I was)
Now I am an adult...Before I was a child.
Now you are an adult...Before you were a child.
Now she is an adult...Before she was a child.

Now there is a problem...Before there was a problem
Now there are books...Before there were no books.

Now I have...Before I used to have (I had)
Now I have the surprise.
Before I didn't have the surprise.
Now Carlos has
Before Carlos used to have
Now Pedro has the surprise.
Before Pedro didn't have the surprise.
Now you have the problem.
Before you didn't have the problem.

Now I want...Before I used to want (I wanted)
Now I want to read.
Before I wanted to read.

Ahora Antonio quiere leer.	Now Antonio wants to read.
Antes José Luis quería leer.	Before José Luis wanted to read.
Ahora Ud. quiere platicar. (2-a)	Now you want to talk.
Antes Ud. quería charlar.	Before you wanted to talk (chat).
Ahora ella quiere conversar.	Now she wants to converse.
Antes ella quería conversar.	Before she wanted to converse.

(Listen to the model)

¿Necesitaba ella el regalo?	Did she need the gift?
--*Sí, ella necesitaba el regalo.*	*Yes, she needed the gift.*
¿Necesitaba Ud. el regalo?	Did you need the gift?
--*Sí, (yo) necesitaba el regalo.*	*Yes, I needed the gift.*

(Answer the questions affirmatively. The correct answer will follow.)

¿Llevaba Carlos a su hija?	Did Carlos used to carry his daughter?
--*Sí, Carlos llevaba a su hija.*	*Yes, Carlos used to carry his daughter.*
¿Llevaba Ud. a la niña?	Did you used to carry the girl?
--*Sí, (yo) llevaba a la niña.*	*Yes, I used to carry the girl.*
¿Era pequeña ella?	Did she used to be little?
--*Sí, ella era pequeña.*	*Yes, she used to be little.*
¿Tenía Carlos la sorpresa?	Did Carlos have the surprise?
--*Sí, Carlos tenía la sorpresa.*	*Yes, Carlos had the surprise.*
¿Quería Ud. hablar?	Did you want to talk?
--*Sí, (yo) quería hablar.*	*Yes, I wanted to talk.*

DIÁLOGO

DIALOG

Una conversación en la oficina de una iglesia. La secretaria habla con el padre Guillermo.(2-b)

A conversation in a church office. The secretary speaks with Father William.

SECRETARIA--Buenas tardes, padre. ¿Cómo está Ud.?

Good afternoon, Father. How are you?

PADRE--Bien, gracias. ¿Y Ud.?

Fine, thanks. And you?

SECRETARIA--Bien. ¿Quiere Ud. un café o prefiere un refresco? Son las cuatro y media.

Fine. Do you want coffee or do you prefer a soft drink? It's 4:30.

VOCABULARY AND CULTURAL NOTES

a) There are several words meaning *to talk or chat:* HABLAR (to speak), CONVERSAR (to converse), CHARLAR (to talk or chat). PLATICAR (to talk) is a favorite among Mexicans. The noun forms are: *una conversación, una charla, una plática.*

b) *el padre Guillermo* (Father William) In Latin America priests are called Father (*padre*) or Brother (*fray*) with the first name. In Spain priests often are called *don* with the first name, as *don Bartolomé.* The article (*el, la*) is used when talking about someone with a title of Mr., Mrs., Father, Dr., etc. The article, which doesn't translate into English, is dropped in direct address (in conversation). Generally, only abbreviated titles are capitalized in Spanish. *Los Sres. (señores) García* = Mr. and Mrs. Garcia

Nuestro sacerdote, el padre Javier, es muy amable. (Our priest, Father Javier, is very kind.)
¿Cómo está Ud., padre Javier? (How are you, Father Javier?---direct address)
La Sra. (señora) García está con nosotros. (Mrs. Garcia is with us.)
Sra. Garcia, ¿cómo están sus hijos? (Mrs. Garcia, how are your children?---direct address)
Quiero hablar con el Dr. (doctor) Pérez. (I want to talk to Dr. Perez.)

IRREGULAR VERBS IN THE IMPERFECT TENSE

	IR--to go	SER--to be	VER--to see	HAY (there is/ there are)
yo	iba	era	veía	HABÍA (there was/ there were)
tú	ibas	eras	veías	
Ud.	iba	era	veía	
nosotros	íbamos	éramos	veíamos	
Uds.	iban	eran	veían	

SOME ADVERBIAL EXPRESSIONS THAT TAKE THE IMPERFECT TENSE

siempre	(always)	a veces	(sometimes)
con frecuencia	(frequently)	muchas veces	(many times, often)
frecuentemente	(frequently)	cada año, día, mes	(every year, day, month)
a menudo	(often)	todos los días	(every day)
de vez en cuando	(once in a while)	todos los lunes	(every Monday)

The imperfect tense is used commonly with MENTAL ACTIVITY IN THE PAST. Such verbs are:
QUERER (to want), PREFERIR (to prefer), SABER (to know), CREER (to believe), PODER (to be able), PENSAR (to think) and DESEAR (to desire or want). The imperfect is also used with TIME and WEATHER.

Ellos querían jugar.	(They wanted/used to want to play.)
Sabíamos la respuesta.	(We knew /used to know the answer.)
Eran las diez de la noche.	(It was 10:00 p.m.)
Hacía buen tiempo.	(The weather was good.)

2-E   PREPOSITIONAL PRONOUNS   Pronouns that follow a preposition are the same as the subject pronouns with the exception of YO and TÚ which change to MÍ and TI.

SUBJECT   PREPOSITIONAL

yo	(I)	mí	(me)	a mí, de mí, para mí, CONMIGO (to me, of me, for me, with me)
tú	(you-fam.)	ti	(you)	a ti, de ti, para ti, CONTIGO (to you-familiar, of you, for you, with you)
él	(he)	él	(he)	a él, de él, para él, con él (to him, of him, for him, with him--NO CONTRACTION)
ella	(she)	ella	(she)	a ella, de ella, para ella, con ella (to her, of her, for her, with her)
Ud.	(you)	Ud.	(you)	a Ud., de Ud., para Ud., con Ud. (to you, of you, for you, with you)
nosotros	(we)	nosotros	(we)	a nosotros, de nosotros, para nosotros, con nosotros (to, of, for, with us)
ellos	(they)	ellos	(they)	a ellos, de ellos, para ellos, con ellos (to, of, for, with them)
ellas	(they)	ellas	(they)	a ellas, de ellas, para ellas, con ellas (to, of, for, with them)
Uds.	(you [pl.])	Uds.	(you [pl.])	a Uds., de Uds., para Uds., con Uds. (to, of, for, with you [pl.])

Now that digital clocks are more common, there are more variations. One might hear 5:45 as *Son las cinco y cuarenta y cinco.*

NOTE that *cuarto* (quarter) is very close to *cuatro* (four). If it causes problems, use the alternate word, *quince.*

¿A QUÉ HORA?   (At what time...?) in a question requires *a* (at) in the answer, exactly as in English.

¿A qué hora es el bautismo?   --El bautismo es a las diez y media. (What time is the baptism?--The baptism is AT 10:30.)

USEFUL PHRASES:

de la mañana // en la mañana   (a.m.--in the morning)
de la tarde // en la tarde   (p.m.--in the afternoon)
de la noche// en la noche   (p.m.--in the evening, night)
mediodía (noon)   medianoche (midnight)   en punto (on the dot)

2-D IMPERFECT TENSE

This past tense in Spanish expresses continuance (actions not completed) and actions in the past that were customary or habitual. It is the most regular verb tense in Spanish with only three irregular verbs: SER, IR, and VER. Sometimes the imperfect is referred to as the *ABA--IA verbs.* It is most often confused with the preterite tense, which is used with completed actions. The best translation in English for the imperfect tense is *used to...*   Other translations are common but may confuse the learner.

yo HABLABA { I used to speak / I was speaking / I spoke

(preterite)
yo HABLÉ-- I spoke, I did speak

	COMPRAR--to buy	COMER--to eat	ESCRIBIR--to write	
yo	compraba	comía	escribía	(I used to buy, eat, write)
tú	comprabas	comías	escribías	(You [fam.] used to buy, eat, write)
Ud.	compraba	comía	escribía	(You used to buy, eat, write)
nosotros	comprábamos	comíamos	escribíamos	(We used to buy, eat, write)
Uds.	compraban	comían	escribían	(You [pl.] used to buy, eat, write)

Since *yo* and *Ud.* have the same endings in the imperfect tense, *you--I* questions and answers are easier because there is no change in the verb.   ¿Trabajaba Ud.?-----Sí, (yo) trabajaba.   (Did you used to work?--Yes, I used to work.)

ANSWERING QUESTIONS   QUESTION-----------ANSWER

¿Tiene Ud.? ----→   (yo) Tengo. (Do **you** have?--**I** have)
¿Tienen Uds.? ---→(nosotros) Tenemos. (Do **you** (all) have?---**We** have)

Other questions and answers are easier because the subject and verb forms are the same.

¿Tiene él?------Él tiene   (Does he have?---He has)
¿Tiene ella?-----Ella tiene   (Does she have?--She has)
¿Tienen ellos?---Ellos tienen (Do they have?--They have)
¿Tienen ellas?---Ellas tienen (Do they have?--They have)
¿Tenemos nosotros?--Nosotros tenemos (Do we have?--We have)

2-B NEGATIVE WORDS

Double negatives are the norm in Spanish. In some cases there are two correct ways of making a negative statement. The most common uses of the negative are:

AFFIRMATIVE   NEGATIVE

Quiero ALGO. (I want something.)   NADA quiero. // NO quiero NADA. (I don't want anything.)
ALGUIEN está. (There is someone.)   NADIE está. // NO está NADIE.   (There is no one.)
SIEMPRE Ana está aquí. (Ana is always here.)   NUNCA está aquí.// NO está aquí NUNCA. (She is never here.)

There can be several negatives in a Spanish sentence.
        NO está aquí NADIE NUNCA. (Nobody is ever here.)

2-C   TELLING TIME

¿QUÉ HORA ES? (What time is it?)   Only 1:00 is seen as singular: ES la una. (It is 1:00.) Es la una y media. (It is 1:30)
                                    Other hours are plural: SON las dos. (It is 2:00) Son las cinco. (It is 5:00.)

Time is added on the right half of the clock with Y (and) subtracted from the next hour on the left half of the clock *menos* (less).

Son las dos y diez. (2:10)   Son las tres y veinte. (3:20)
Son las tres y CUARTO. (3:15) // Son las tres y quince. (3:15)
Son las cinco y MEDIA. (6:30) // Son las cinco y treinta. (6:30)
Son las tres MENOS diez. (2:50)
Son las seis menos cuarto (5:45) // Son las seis menos quince. (5:45)

Chapter 2 - "SWEET 15" OR QUINCEAÑERA   **26**

PRESENT TENSE REGULAR VERBS

	NECESITAR	COMER	VIVIR	
yo	necesito	como	vivo	
tú	necesitas	comes	vives	
Ud. él ella	necesita	come	vive	(In later chapters this form will be introduced by Ud.)
nosotros	necesitamos	comemos	vivimos	
Uds. ellos ellas	necesitan	comen	viven	(In later chapters this form will be introduced by Uds.)

Yo, tú and *nosotros* are usually dropped as subjects because the meaning is clear by the verb ending. *Ud.* may be dropped when the meaning is evident in a *You-I* conversation. Too much repetition of *yo* sounds boastful to the Spanish ear. Other subject pronouns generally are used.

VIVO
- I live
- I do live
- I am living

The present tense in Spanish takes on a broader sense than in English. The *do/does* translation is used most often in questions:
¿Vivo aquí? (Do I live here?)
The present progressive tense (see Chapter 11) translates as I *am living* but is used far less than the present tense.

Many of the most useful verbs in Spanish are somewhat or very irregular in the present tense. Sometimes it is easier to memorize a few forms than trying to learn all the *whys*. PASTORAL SPANISH uses irregular verbs from the beginning but limits the persons to mostly *yo, Ud., él, ella* forms. When possible the program teaches phrases that use infinitives to quickly expand vocabulary. Each chapter reviews some verbs along with vocabulary but material builds up very quickly.

SOME IRREGULAR PRESENT TENSE VERBS

	TENER (to have)	SER (to be)	QUERER (to want)	PREFERIR (to prefer)
yo	tengo	soy	quiero	prefiero
tú	tienes	eres	quieres	prefieres
Ud. él ella	tiene	es	quiere	prefiere
nosotros	tenemos	somos	queremos	preferimos
Uds. ellos ellas	tienen	son	quieren	prefieren

SEÑORA--Es muy sencilla. ¿No recuerda Ud. la quinceañera de la hija de los Sánchez del año pasado?

That is simple. Don't you remember the "sweet 15" party of the Sanchez's daughter last year?

PADRE--Sí, recuerdo perfectamente. No fue buena idea. La situación económica es mala y hay muchos sin trabajo. Gastar mucho dinero en una fiesta es un escándalo.

Yes, I remember very well. It wasn't a good idea. The economic situation is bad and many are without work. To spend so much money on a party is a scandal.

SEÑORA--Sí, tiene razón. Pero por lo menos queremos una misa y música.

Yes, you are right. But at least we want a mass and music.

PADRE--Desde luego. Pero lo más importante es la preparación espiritual de su hija.

Of course. But the most important thing is the spiritual preparation of your daughter.

SEÑORA--Entonces, ¿qué necesitamos hacer?

So, what do need to do?

PADRE--Primero, la quinceañera y los padrinos necesitan asistir a una charla (plática). Después tenemos otra charla con la quinceañera y los chambelanes.

First, the birthday girl and the sponsors need to attend a talk. Later we will have another talk with the birthday girl and the escorts.

GRAMMAR

2-A PRONOUNS AND VERBS

Subject pronouns:

yo (I)	nosotros (we)
tú (you)	vosotros (Uds. in Latin America)
él (he)	ellos (they)
ella (she)	ellas (they)
usted (you)	ustedes (you--plural)

NOTE: *tú* and *vosotros* will not be used in exercises in PASTORAL SPANISH I
tú= you (familiar [fam.])
usted=you (more formal)

Infinitives are verbs in *neutral*. Only when conjugated can they *move* by telling us subject, tense and mood.

trabajar = to work
comer = to eat
vivir = to live

PADRE--Normalmente prefiero café pero ahora quiero algo frío--un refresco, gracias.

Normally I prefer coffee but now I want something cold--a soft drink, thanks.

(La secretaria regresa con el refresco)
PADRE--Gracias, muy amable.

(The secretary returns with a soft drink)
Thanks, very kind (of you).

SECRETARIA--De nada, padre.

It's nothing, Father.

PADRE-- ¿Hay correo o recados?

Is there mail or are there messages?

SECRETARIA--Aquí Ud. tiene las cartas. Llamó la Sra. García. Quiere hablar con Ud. (2-E) Favor de llamarla hoy. Aquí está su número de teléfono.

Here you have the letters. Mrs. Garcia called. She wants to talk with you. Please call her today. Here is her telephone number.

(El sacerdote marca el número.)
SEÑORA--Aló (bueno) (dígame)

(The priest dials the number.)
Hello (variations of the greeting)

PADRE--Buenas tardes. Habla el padre Guillermo de Santa Rita. ¿Está la Sra. García? (¿Hablo con la Sra. García?) (2-b)

Good afternoon, Father William speaking from the Church of St. Rita. Is Mrs. Garcia there? (Am I speaking with Mrs. Garcia?)

SEÑORA--Sí, padrecito. Soy yo, Isabel García. Mi esposo y yo queremos pedirle un favor. Nuestra hija va a cumplir quince años y nos gustaría celebrar su cumpleaños.

Yes, Father. It's me, Isabel Garcia. My husband and I want you to do us a favor. Our daughter is going to be 15 and we would like to celebrate her birthday.

PADRE--Sí, cómo no. ¿Para qué me necesitan Uds.?

Yes, why not? What do you need me for?

SEÑORA--Bueno, es nuestra costumbre celebrar la quinceañera con una misa y fiesta y todo.

Well, it is our custom to celebrate with a Mass and party and everything.

PADRE--Sí, yo sé. Pero es mejor hacerlo sencillo y no gastar tanto dinero.

Yes, I know. But it is better to do it simply and not spent so much money.

SEÑORA--Precisamente, Padre Guillermo. Quisiéramos solamente ocho chambelanes, cuatro padrinos y una banda.

Precisely, Father William. We would like only eight escorts, four sponsors and a band.

PADRE-- ¿Cómo? ¡Eso es una fiesta enorme!

What? That is a huge party!

CHAPTER 3

WEDDING

TAPESCRIPT

(Listen and repeat)

¿Qué necesita Ud.?
--Necesito saber algo.
--No necesito saber nada.
¿Qué sabe Ud? (3-A)
-- (yo) sé muchas cosas.
--No sé.
--No sé nada.
--Sé que...
El matrimonio es un sacramento.
Sé que el matrimonio es un sacramento.
El matrimonio requiere (3-a)
                la responsabilidad.

Sé que...
Sé que el matrimonio requiere la responsabilidad.
¿Quién sabe? (1-E)
--(yo) sé.
--No sé. Dios sabe.
¿Quién sabe?
--Paco sabe.
--Luisa sabe.
--Ud. sabe.
--Ellos saben.
--Uds. saben.

What do you need?
I need to know something.
I don't need to know anything.
What do you know?
I know many things.
I don't know.
I don't know anything.
I know that...
Marriage is a sacrament.
I know that marriage is a sacrament.
Marriage requires
                responsibility.
I know that...
I know that marriage requires responsibility.
Who knows?
I know.
I don't know. God knows.
Who knows?
Paco knows.
Luisa knows.
You know.
They know.
You (pl.) know.

(nosotros) sabemos.
Paco y yo sabemos.
¿SABE UD.? --Sí, (yo) SÉ.
¿SABEN UDS.? --Sí, SABEMOS.
Sabemos que...
Es importante.
Sabemos que es importante.
Es posible.
Sabemos que es posible.
Dios es justo.
Sabemos que Dios es justo.
El anillo es de oro.
Sabemos que el anillo es de oro.
El matrimonio requiere
          la fidelidad. (3-b)
Sabemos que el matrimonio requiere la fidelidad.
El matrimonio requiere la madurez.
Sabemos que el matrimonio requiere la madurez.
Sabemos unas cosas.
Sabemos HACER unas cosas.
¿Qué sabe hacer Ud?
--(yo) Sé manejar.
--Sé manejar un coche (un carro). (3-c)
--Sé escribir.
--Sé leer.
--Sé hablar un poco de español. (3-d)
--Sé hacer el café.

We know.
Paco and I know.
Do YOU know? Yes, I know.
Do you (all) know? Yes, WE know.
We know that...
It is important.
We know that it is important.
It is possible.
We know that it is possible.
God is just.
We know that God is just.
The ring is gold (of gold).
We know that the ring is gold.
Marriage requires
          fidelity.
We know that marriage requires fidelity.
Marriage requires maturity.
We know that marriage requires maturity.
We know some things.
We know how TO DO some things.
What do you know how to do?
I know how to drive.
I know how to drive a car.
I know how to write.
I know how to read.
I know how to speak a little Spanish.
I know how to make coffee.

(Answer the question with the new subject. After a pause the correct answer will be given)

¿Quién sabe hablar inglés?
Paco ...(*Paco sabe hablar inglés.*)
Ud.... (*Ud. sabe hablar inglés.*)
Yo... (*Sé hablar inglés.*)
Nosotros...(*Sabemos hablar inglés.*)
Ellos...(*Ellos saben hablar inglés.*)

Who knows how to speak English?
Paco...(*Paco knows how to speak English.*)
You...(*You know how to speak English.*)
I ...(*I know how to speak English.*)
We...(*We know how to speak English.*)
They...(*They know how to speak English.*)

(Listen and repeat)

Ahora (yo) SÉ......Antes (yo) SABÍA. (3-B)	Now I know...Before I knew (used to know).
Ahora sé manejar...Antes sabía manejar.	Now I know how to drive..Before I knew how to drive.
Ahora Ud. sabe...Antes Ud. sabía.	Now you know...Before you knew (used to know).
Ahora ella sabe...Antes ella sabía.	Now she knows...Before she knew.
Ahora Uds. SABEN...Antes Uds. SABÍAN.	Now you (all) know...Before you knew.
Ahora SABEMOS...Antes SABÍAMOS.	Now we know...Before we knew.
Ahora ES importante.	Now it is important.
Antes ERA importante. (3-C)	Before it was important.
Antes era posible.	Before it was possible.
Paco SABÍA que ERA posible.	Paco knew that it was possible.
(yo) Sabía que era posible.	I knew that it was possible.
Ella sabía que era importante.	She knew that it was important.

(Substitute the new subjects in the sentences. The correct answer will follow the pause.)

Mi madre sabía que era importante. (Carlos)	My mother knew that it was important. (Carlos)
Carlos sabía que era importante. (nosotros)	*Carlos knew it was important.* (We)
Sabíamos que era importante. (Ud.)	*We knew it was important.* (You)
Ud sabía que era importante. (yo)	*You knew that it was important.* (I)
Sabía que era importante. (ellos)	*I knew it was important.* (they)
Ellos sabían que era importante. (la novia) (3-e)	*They knew it was important.* (the bride)
La novia sabía que era importante. (los esposos)	*The bride knew it was important.* (the spouses)
Los esposos sabían que era importante.	*The spouses knew it was important.*

(Repetición)

(Repetition)

Necesito CREER. (3-D)	I need to believe.
(yo) CREO.	I believe.
Creo en Dios.	I believe in God.
Creo que sí.	I believe so.
Dios es todopoderoso.	God is omnipotent.
Creo que...	I believe that...
Creo que Dios es todopoderoso.	I believe that God is omnipotent.
Mi familia es importante.	My family is important.
Creo que mi familia es importante.	I believe that my family is important.
Es verdad.	It is true.
Anita CREE que...	Anita believes that...

Anita cree que es verdad.	Anita believes that it is true.
Es falso...Es mentira.	It is false...It is a lie.
Anita cree que es falso.	Anita believes it is false.
Anita cree que es mentira.	Anita believes it is a lie.
Su novio es fiel.	Her boyfriend is faithful.
Anita cree que su novio es fiel.	Anita believes that her boyfriend is faithful.
Ellos CREEN que...	They believe that...
Es un amor verdadero.	It is (a) true love.
Ellos creen que es un amor verdadero.	They believe that it is true love.
CREEMOS en Dios.	We believe in God.
Creemos que es verdad.	We believe that it is true.
Ahora (3-f)(yo) CREO...Antes CREÍA.	Now I believe...Before I believed (used to believe).
Ahora Ud cree..Antes Ud creía.	Now you believe...Before you believed.
Ahora (nosotros) CREEMOS...Antes CREÍAMOS.	Now we believe...Before we believed.
Ahora ellos CREEN...Antes ellos CREÍAN.	Now they believe...Before they believed.

(Substitute with the new subject. The correct answer will follow.)

(yo) Creía que era verdad. (el novio)	I believed that it was true. (the groom)
El novio creía que era verdad. (los esposos)	The groom believed that it was true. (the spouses)
Los esposos creían que era verdad. (mi padre)	The spouses believed it was true. (my father)
Mi padre creía que era verdad. (nosotros)	My father believed that it was true. (we)
Creíamos que era verdad. (los padrinos)	We believed that it was true. (the godparents)
Los padrinos creían que era verdad.	The godparents believed that it was true.

CONOCER   (3-E) | TO KNOW (PEOPLE)

(Repetición) | (Repetition)

CONOZCO a Carlos. (3-F)	I know Carlos.
Carlos CONOCE a María.	Carlos knows Maria.
Carlos y María CONOCEN a Carmen.	Carlos and Maria know Carmen.
También	Also
También conozco a Carmen.	I also know Carmen.
CONOCEMOS a Felipe.	We know Felipe.
También Ud conoce a Felipe.	You also know Felipe.
Ahora (yo) CONOZCO...Antes CONOCÍA.	Now I know...Before I knew (with people).
Ahora Carlos CONOCE...Antes Carlos CONOCÍA.	Now Carlos knows...Before Carlos knew.
Ahora CONOCEMOS...Antes CONOCÍAMOS.	Now we know...Before we knew.

Ahora ellos CONOCEN...Antes ellos CONOCÍAN.   Now they know...Before they knew.

COMPARING SABER---CONOCER

(Listen and repeat)

Conozco a Carlos.	I know Carlos.
Sé que Carlos es el esposo de María.	I know that Carlos is Maria's husband.
María sabe que Ana tiene tres hijos.	Maria knows that Ana has 3 children.
María conoce a Ana pero no conoce a sus hijos.	Maria knows Ana but not her children.
Carmen no sabe manejar.	Carmen doesn't know how to drive.

¿Se conocen Uds. desde hace mucho tiempo?	Have you known each other a long time?
--Nos conocemos desde hace años.	We've known each other for years.
--Somos novios desde hace años.	We've been going together for years.
--Nos conocimos	We met
el año pasado.	last year.
hace un año.	a year ago.
hace seis meses.	6 months ago.
¿Quieren Uds. casarse?	Do you want to get married (to each other)?
--Queremos casarnos pronto.	We want to get married soon.
en tres meses.	in 3 months.
en el verano.	in the summer.
--Queremos casarnos en octubre.	We want to get married in October.
el año que viene.	next year.
el próximo año.	next year.
Queremos preparar la ceremonia.	We want to plan the ceremony.
una boda grande.	a big wedding.
invitar a muchos amigos.	to invite lots of friends.
.¿Cuándo quieren Uds. tener el ensayo?	When do you want to have the rehearsal?
--Queremos el ensayo el tres de abril.	We want the rehearsal on April 3.
¿Tienen Uds. el padrino de la boda?	Do you have the bestman?
la dama de honor?	the maid of honor?
las damas?	the bridesmaids?
los chambelanes?	ushers (escorts) ?
los pajes?	ring bearer, flower girl?
¿Quieren Uds. escoger	Do you want to chose
la música?	the music?
la selección del Antiguo Testamento?	the Old Testament reading?

Los esposos se quieren
en la enfermedad
en la salud
en la prosperidad

The spouses love each other.
in sickness
in health
in prosperity

(Listen and repeat)

Ahora Ud quiere...Antes Ud quería
Ud. quería hablar con el sacerdote.
(yo) quería hablar con los novios.
La dama de honor quería rezar.
La madre de la novia quería escoger un vestido.
La abuela quería comprar las flores.

Now you want...Before you wanted
You wanted to speak with the priest.
I wanted to speak to the bride and groom.
The bridesmaid wanted to pray.
The mother of the bride wanted to chose a dress.
The grandmother wanted to buy the flowers.

PODER   (3-G)
(yo) PUEDO
Puedo manejar un coche.
Sé manejar un coche.
Puedo preparar la ceremonia.
Puedo comprar los regalos.
Ud. PUEDE
ella puede
(nosotros) PODEMOS
Ellos PUEDEN
Uds. pueden recibir las cartas.

TO BE ABLE, CAN
I can
I can (am able) to drive a car.
I know how to drive a car.
I can prepare the ceremony.
I can buy the gifts.
You can
She can
We can
They can
You (all) can receive the letters.

UNAS FRASES PARA EXPRESAR LA OBLIGACIÓN (3-H)

SOME PHRASES TO EXPRESS OBLIGATION

(yo) TENGO QUE
Ud. tiene que practicar.
Uds. TIENEN QUE recibir las cartas.
Uds. NECESITAN recibir las cartas.
HAY QUE recibir las cartas.   (3-I)
Uds. DEBEN recibir las cartas.
DEBER
(yo) DEBO ayudar.
Debo escoger la música.
Debo preparar la comida.
Ud. DEBE estudiar.

I have to (must)
You have to practice.
You have to (must) receive the letters.
You need to receive the letters.
One must (impersonal subject) receive the letters.
You ought to (should) receive the letters.
TO OUGHT
I ought to help.
I ought to chose the music.
I ought to prepare the meal.
You ought to study.

(nosotros) DEBEMOS escuchar las cintas.	We ought to listen to the tapes.
Uds. DEBEN descansar.	You ought to rest.
el deber	the obligation (noun)
todos los días	every day

UNOS DEBERES DE LOS CRISTIANOS

SOME OBLIGATIONS OF CHRISTIANS

Debemos rezar.
We ought to pray.

Debemos rezar todos los días.
We ought to pray every day.

Debemos amar a Dios   con todo nuestro ser
We ought to love God   with all our being (might).

Debemos amar a Dios con todo nuestro ser.
We ought to love God with all our might.

Debemos rezar por nosotros mismos,
We ought to pray for ourselves,
      por la familia,
         for our family,
      por amigos y vecinos,
         for friends and neighbors,
      por los obispos, sacerdotes y religiosos,
         for bishops, priests and religious
      y aun por nuestros enemigos.
         and even for our enemies.

Debemos hablar con respeto
We ought to speak with respect
   de personas, lugares y cosas santas.
   of people, places and holy matters(things).

UNAS FRASES ESPECIALES PARA UNA BODA

SPECIAL PHRASES FOR A WEDDING

¡Felicitaciones!
Congratulations!

¡Que Dios los bendiga!
May God bless you (both)!

Espero que Dios les dé la felicidad.
I hope God grants you happiness.
      les dé la salud.
         grants you health.
      les dé el amor de la parroquia.
         grants you the love of the parish.

Espero que los nuevos esposos sean felices para siempre.
I hope the new spouses are happy forever.
         sean fieles para siempre.
            are faithful forever.
         sean fuertes para siempre.
            are strong forever.

DIÁLOGO: MARTA Y SU NOVIO HABLAN DEL MATRIMONIO CON EL SACERDOTE

MARTA --Buenas tardes, padre. Quiero presentarle a Santiago Jiménez, mi novio.
Good afternoon, Father. I want to introduce you to my boyfriend, Santiago Jimenez.

PADRE --Mucho gusto. (Le da la mano.)
It's a pleasure.   (He shakes hands.)

NOVIO --Mucho gusto. Marta y su familia hablan mucho
It's a pleasure. My fiancee and her family talk a lot about

de Ud., padre. Marta y yo nos conocimos hace un año y queremos planear nuestra boda.

you, Father. Marta and I met a year ago and we want to plan our wedding.

PADRE -- ¿Cuándo quieren casarse?

When do you want to get married?

MARTA --Queremos casarnos en abril, en seis meses. Quisiéramos una boda grande con muchas flores y muchos invitados.

We want to get married in April, in six months. We would like a big wedding with lots of flowers and many guests.

PADRE --Sé que Marta es soltera. Es su primer matrimonio, Santiago, ¿ no es verdad? ¿Es Ud. católico?

I know that Marta is single. It is your first marriage isn't it? Are you Catholic?

NOVIO --Sí, soy soltero. No soy casado. Soy católico. Nací en Puerto Rico y me bautizaron allí, pero vivo en los Estados Unidos desde 1970. Vivo con mi familia en Beacon.

Yes, I'm single. I am not married. I am Catholic. I was born in Puerto Rico and they baptized me there but I've lived in the U.S. since 1970. I live with my family in Beacon.

PADRE --Conozco bien a Marta y a su familia. Quiero conocer a Ud. también. ¿Cuántos años tiene Ud? ¿Tiene Ud. hermanos? ¿Dónde trabaja?

I know Marta and her family well. I want to know you also. How old are you? Do you have brothers (and sisters)? Where do you work?

NOVIO --Tengo veinticinco años--tres más que Marta. Tengo un hermano y dos hermanas. Soy mecánico en Firestone. Mi trabajo es estable.

I am 25--three years older than Marta. I have one brother and two sisters. I am a mechanic at Firestone. My work (job) is stable.

PADRE --Muy bien. Uds. saben que el matrimonio es un sacramento. Es una unión para toda la vida. Deben saber que es un paso serio que requiere responsibilidad, fidelidad y madurez.

Very good. You know that marriage is a sacrament. It is a union for life. You ought to know that it is a serious step that requires responsibility, fidelity and maturity.

NOVIO --Comprendemos la importancia y por eso queremos hablar con Ud. Creo que tenemos un amor verdadero.

We understand the importance and for that reason we want to talk to you. We believe ours is a true love.

MARTA --Nos queremos y nos respetamos. Tenemos muchos intereses en común. Adoramos a los niños y queremos una familia.

We love and respect each other. We have many interests in common. We adore children and want a family.

PADRE --Me alegro mucho y los felicito. La Iglesia tiene un equipo de personas que preparan a las parejas para el matrimonio.

That makes me happy and I congratulate you. The Church has a has a team to prepare couples for marriage. One must

Hay que fijar las fechas para las charlas (pláticas) prematri-moniales. Es un día de reflexión y recogimiento. Si Uds. quieren, podemos tener un ensayo antes de la boda. Una cosa importante: necesito el certificado de bautismo de Uds. seis meses antes de la boda. También necesito los nombres del padrino, la dama de honor, los chambela-nes, etc. Ahora quiero hablar con cada uno de Uds. a solas.

set the dates for the pre-nuptial talks. It is a day for reflection and circumspection. If you want, we can have a rehearsal before the wedding. Something important: I need your baptismal certificates six months before the wedding. Also I need the names of the best man, the maid of honor, the ushers, etc. Now I want to speak to each of you separately.

MARTA -¡Dios mío! ¡Hay tantos detalles! ¡Yo no sabía!

My goodness! There are so many details! I had no idea!

GRAMMAR

3-A SABER--to know information   Sabemos el número. (We know the number.)
     --to know how to do something   El sabe manejar.   (He knows how to drive.)
     --to know that (indirect discourse) Sabemos que es verdad (We know that it is true / We know it is true.)

Note that in the last sentence English is more flexible than Spanish. The word *que* must always be present in Spanish but *that* can be eliminated in English with no change in meaning.

Present tense	SABER		Imperfect tense		
yo	sé		yo	sabía	(I know---I used to know)
tú	sabes		tú	sabías	(You [fam.] know---used to know)
Ud, él, ella	sabe		Ud, él, ella	sabía	(You, he, she knows---used to know)
nosotros	sabemos		nosotros	sabíamos	(We know---used to know)
Uds, ellos, ellas	saben		Uds, ellos, ellas	sabían	(You [pl.], they know---used to know)

3-B Saber is more commonly used in the imperfect tense than the preterite.   SABÍA is the same form for first and third person singular. (yo SABÍA, Ud. SABÍA) This makes *you--I* question-answers much easier. (SABÍA Ud?--Sí, yo SABÍA) All imperfect forms, whether -ABA or -ÍA ending, have the same form for *yo* and *Ud.*

3-C IMPERSONAL PHRASES   These very useful phrases do not require a subject as they would in English.

Es importante.   Era importante.   Other examples: Es posible.   (It is possible.)
(It is important   (It was important.)   Es imposible.   (It is impossible.)
                                                                  Es verdad.   (It is true.)

3-D CREER --to believe   This verb is conjugated exactly as the verb LEER (to read)

Present tense   **Imperfect tense**
yo   creo   creía
tú   crees   creías   CREER QUE--to believe that
Ud.   cree   creía   Creo que es importante. (I believe that it is important.)
nosotros creemos   creíamos
Uds.   creen   creían

3-E CONOCER --to know people, to be acquainted   (Saber is NEVER used with people.)

Present tense   **Imperfect tense**
yo   conozco   conocía
tú   conoces   conocías
Ud.   conoce   conocía
nosotros conocemos   conocíamos
Uds.   conocen   conocían

3-F PERSONAL a

This unique part of Spanish grammar distinguishes between people and things. **It does not translate into English.** It will become clearer as more verbs are learned. Some examples:

Conozco a Carlos.   (I know Carlos.)
Escuchamos a Ud.   (We listen to you.)   BUT   Escuchamos la música. (We listen to the music.)
Ellos ven a Elena.   (They see Elena.)   BUT   Ellos ven el coche.   (They see the car.) No personal "a"

3-G PODER--to be able, can

This verb usually is followed by an infinitive.

	Present tense	Imperfect tense
yo	puedo	podía
tú	puedes	podías
Ud.	puede	podía
nosotros	podemos	podíamos
Uds.	pueden	podían

Susana puede leer. (Susana can [is able to] read.)
Susana podía leer. (Susana could [was able to] read.)

3-H VERBS TO INDICATE OBLIGATION

NECESITAR--to need	Necesito firmar el documento.	(I need to sign the document.)
TENER QUE--to have to, must	Tengo que escribir las cartas.	(I must write the letters.)
HAY QUE-- one must	Hay que descansar.	(One must rest.) NOTE: this phrase NEVER takes a
DEBER (de)--to ought to	Debo (de) estudiar ahora.	(I ought to study now.) subject.

VOCABULARY AND CULTURAL NOTES

a) *requerer--requiere* (requier) This verb works exactly as the verb QUERER (Chapter 2).

b) *la fidelidad*--(fidelity) All words in Spanish that end in --DAD or --TAD are feminine and mean *-ity* in English.
There are many cognates of this type related to religion, many having their origin in Latin. A few are:

la responsibildad (responsibility)   la comunidad (community)   la sociedad (society)
la prosperidad (prosperity)   la universidad (university)   la felicidad (happiness)

c) *manejar* (to drive or manage) There are several words commonly used in Spanish for *to drive*: MANEJAR, GUIAR and
CONDUCIR. There are also several words for car, some harder to pronounce than others: *el coche, el auto, el automóvil. El carro,*
common in Latin America for *car*, in Spain means *cart*. The word *la máquina,* usually meaning *machine* sometimes
is used to means *car* (especially among Cubans).

---

d) *el inglés* (English--language) Languages in Spanish are always masculine and are not capitalized. Some languages one might refer to are: *el francés* (French); *el español* (Spanish); *el alemán* (German); *el latín* (Latin); *el italiano* (Italian). *Latino* does not mean *Latin* or *Roman*. *Latino* or *hispano* means *Hispanic*. A parishioner could be bilingual (*bilingüe*) in Spanish / English or *español/quechua* or any other of the many Indian languages in Latin America.

e) *novia--novio* Dating can be quite serious in many Spanish-speaking countries. *Novio* (boyfriend) is not usually a casual date. The word often means *engaged to be married* or *bridegroom*. *Novia* is the feminine form.

f) *ahora* (now) *Ahora mismo* (right now) is used with the present progressive tense (Chapter 11). How people relate to time is cultural and varies between countries and social classes in the Spanish-speaking world. *Ahorita* in Honduras means *right away*, but in the Dominican Republic or Mexico could mean a wait of a few hours.

CHAPTER 4

A HAPPY OCCASION: THE NEW YEAR

TAPESCRIPT

(Listen and repeat)

ME GUSTA   (4-A)
         el libro.
         la silla nueva.
         mi pluma azul.

I like (it)
         the book.
         the new chair.
         my blue pen.

¿LE GUSTA el chocolate?
--Sí, me gusta el chocolate.
--Sí, me gusta.
--No, no me gusta el chocolate.
--No, no me gusta.
¿LE GUSTA? --Sí, ME GUSTA.

Do you like chocolate?
Yes, I like chocolate.
Yes, I like it.
No, I don't like chocolate.
No, I don't like it.
Do you like it?   Yes, I like it.

(Answer affirmatively, first in the longer form, then in the shorter one. The anwers will follow.)

¿Le gusta la fiesta?
--Sí, me gusta la fiesta.
--Sí, me gusta.

Do you like the party?
Yes, I like the party.
Yes, I like it.

¿Le gusta el coche?
--Sí, me gusta el coche.
--Sí, me gusta.

Do you like the car?
Yes, I like the car.
Yes, I like it.

¿Le gusta el anillo?	Do you like the ring?
--Sí, me gusta el anillo.	Yes, I like the ring.
--Sí, me gusta.	Yes I like it.
¿Le gusta la fruta?	Do you like fruit?
--Sí, me gusta la fruta.	Yes, I like fruit.
--Sí, me gusta.	Yes, I like it.

(Listen and repeat)

Me gusta el libro.	I like the book.
ME GUSTAN los libros.	I like (the) books.
Me gusta la casa.	I like the house.
Me gustan las casas.	I like (the) houses.
Me gusta la película.	I like the film.
Me gustan las películas.	I like (the) films.
¿ Le gustan los regalos?	Do you like (the) gifts?
--Sí, me gustan los regalos.	Yes, I like (the) gifts.
--Sí, me gustan.	Yes, I like them.

(Answer affirmatively, first in the longer form, later in the shorter form. The answers will follow.)

¿Le gustan los deportes?	Do you like sports?
--*Sí, me gustan los deportes.*	*Yes, I like sports.*
--*Sí, me gustan.*	*Yes, I like them.*
¿Le gustan las películas?	Do you like films?
--*Sí, me gustan las películas.*	*Yes, I like films.*
--*Sí, me gustan.*	*Yes, I like them.*
¿Le gustan las canciones?	Do you like the songs?
--*Sí, me gustan las canciones.*	*Yes, I like the songs.*
--*Sí, me gustan.*	*Yes, I like them.*

(Listen and repeat)

Me gusta el chocolate---Me gusta COMER el chocolate.	I like chocolate--I like to eat chocolate.
Me gusta leer libros.	I like to read books (reading books).
Me gusta conversar con mi hermano.	I like to converse with my brother.

Chapter 4 - A HAPPY OCCASION: THE NEW YEAR

Me gusta hablar por teléfono.	I like to talk on the phone.
Me gusta rezar en la iglesia.	I like to pray in church.
Me gusta explicar los sacramentos.	I like to explain the sacraments.
Me gusta aprender algo nuevo.	I like to learn something new.
Me gusta conocer a la gente.	I like to meet people.
Me gusta jugar al fútbol. (4-a)	I like to play soccer.
No me gusta escribir a máquina.	I don't like to type.
No me gusta manejar mi coche.	I don't like to drive my car.
No me gusta matar mosquitos.	I don't like to kill mosquitos.
A Ud. LE gusta conversar.	You like to converse.
A Carlos LE gusta charlar.	Carlos likes to talk.
A Marta LE gusta platicar.	Marta likes to talk.
A Uds. LES gusta leer.	You (pl.) like to read.
A Carlos y Roberto LES gusta enseñar.	Carlos and Roberto like to teach.
A los niños LES gusta jugar.	The children like to play.
(a mí) ME gusta dormir.	I like to sleep.
(a nosotros) NOS gusta escuchar las cintas.	We like to listen to the tapes.
Nos gusta escuchar música.	We like to listen to music.
Nos gusta escuchar a Marta.	We like to listen to Marta.
Nos gusta preparar la lección. (4-b)	We like to prepare the lesson.

(Substitute the new subject. The answer will follow the pause)

A Carlos le gusta la lección--A Marta--	Carlos likes the lesson--Marta
A Marta le gusta la lección--Al señor--	*Marta likes the lesson*--The man
Al señor le gusta la lección--A ellos	*The man likes the lesson*--They
A ellos les gusta la lección--A mí--	*They like the lesson*--I
(a mí) *Me gusta la lección*--A Ud.--	*I like the lesson*--You
A Ud. le gusta la lección--A nosotros	*You like the lesson* --We
(a nosotros) *Nos gusta la lección.*	*We like the lesson.*

(Answer the question using the new infinitive. The correct answer will follow.)

A Carlos ¿qué le gusta hacer los lunes? (enseñar)	What does Carlos like to do on Mondays? (teach)
--*A Carlos le gusta enseñar los lunes.*	*Carlos likes to teach on Mondays.*
A Carlos ¿qué le gusta hacer los martes? (dormir)	What does Carlos like to do on Tuesdays? (sleep)
--*A Carlos le gusta dormir los martes.*	*Carlos likes to sleep on Tuesdays.*

A Carlos ¿qué le gusta hacer los sábados? (bailar)
--A Carlos le gusta bailar los sábados.
A Carlos ¿qué le gusta hacer durante el fin de semana? (cantar)
--A Carlos le gusta cantar durante el fin de semana.

What does Carlos like to do on Saturdays? (dance)
Carlos likes to dance on Saturday.
What does Carlos like to do during the weekend? (sing)
Carlos likes to sing during the weekend.

INDIRECT OBJECT PRONOUNS WITH OTHER VERBS

(Listen and repeat)

EXPLICAR
(yo) Explico el problema.
Ud. explica el problema.
Ana ME explica el problema (a mí).
Ana ME explica el problema.
Pablo NOS explica el problema (a nosotros).
Pablo NOS explica el problema.
ENSEÑAR
(yo) Enseño la solución.
Ud. enseña la solución.
Ana ME enseña las soluciones.
Ana NOS enseña las soluciones.

LE—{ a Ud. / a ella / a él

Pablo ME explica el problema.
Pablo LE explica el problema a Ud.
Pablo LE explica el problema a ella.
Pablo LE explica el problema a él.

(yo) LE enseño la lección a la niña.
LE enseño la lección al señor.
LE enseño la lección a Ud.

DAR
DOY
Doy una fiesta.
Ud. DA   él DA   ella DA
(nosotros) DAMOS   él y yo DAMOS

TO EXPLAIN
I explain the problem.
You explain the problem.
Ana explains the problem to me.
 "   "   "   "   "
Pablo explains the problem to us.
 "   "   "   "   "

TO TEACH
I teach the solution.
You teach the solution.
Ana teaches me (to me) the solutions.
Ana teaches us (to us) the solutions.

to you, to her, to him (indirect object pronoun)

Pablo explains the problem to me.
Pablo explains the problem to you.
Pablo explains the problem to her.
Pablo explains the problem to him.

I teach the lesson to the girl.
I teach the lesson to the man.
I teach the lesson to you.

TO GIVE
I give
I give a party.
You give   he gives   she gives
We give   He and I give

Uds. DAN   ellos DAN   ellas DAN

(yo) Le doy el dinero a Ud.
Ud. me da el dinero.
No le doy el dinero a mi hermano.
Carlos no me da el dinero.
Ellos me dan el regalo.
Ellos nos dan el regalo.
Ellos le dan el regalo a la abuela.
Les damos las velas a ellos.
Les damos las velas a Uds.
No les damos las velas a los hombres.

DECIR
(yo) DIGO
Siempre digo la verdad.
Ud. DICE   él DICE   ella DICE
La hermana me dice muchas cosas.
Yo le digo muchas cosas a ella.
(nosotros) DECIMOS
Nunca decimos mentiras.
Uds. DICEN   ellos DICEN   ellas DICEN
Le digo la verdad { a Ud. / a Jorge. / a mi madre. }
Ellos me dicen algo interesante.
Les decimos algo a ellos.
No le digo nada a Jorge.
Jorge no me dice nada tampoco.

You (pl.) give   they give

I give the money to you (give you the money).
You give me the money (the money to me).
I don't give the money to my brother.
Carlos doesn't give the money to me.
They give the gift to me.
They give the gift to us.
They give the gift to the grandmother.
We give the candles to them.
We give the candles to you (pl.).
We don't give the candles to the men.

TO SAY (or tell)
I say
I always say the truth.
You say   He says   She says
The sister tells many things to me.
I tell many things to her.
We say
We never say (tell) lies.
You (pl.) say   they say
I tell the truth { to you. / to Jorge. / to my mother. }
They tell something interesting to me.
We tell something to them.
I don't tell anything to Jorge.
Jorge doesn't tell anything to me either.

(Reply affirmatively to the question. The correct answer follows. First listen to the model.)

Model: hablar   ¿Habla Ud. inglés?
(*Sí, hablo inglés.*)

escuchar   ¿Escucha Ud. las cintas? (4-c)
(*Sí, escucho las cintas.*)
esperar   ¿Espera Ud. a los García?
(*Sí, espero a los García.*)

to speak   Do you speak English?
(*Yes, I speak English.*)

to listen (to)   Do you listen to the tapes?
(*Yes, I listen to the tapes.*)
to wait (for)   Are You waiting for Mr. and Mrs. Garcia?
(*Yes, I am waiting for Mr. and Mrs. Garcia.*)

buscar   ¿Busca Ud. una buena solución?
(*Sí, busco una buena solución.*)
to look (for) Are you looking for a good solution?
(*Yes, I'm looking for a good solution.*)

hacer unas preguntas   ¿Hace Ud. unas preguntas?
(*Sí, hago unas preguntas.*)
to ask question   Do you ask questions?
(*Yes, I ask questions.*)

comprender   ¿Comprende Ud. las respuestas?
(*Sí, comprendo las respuestas.*)
to understand   Do you understand the answers?
(*Yes, I understand the answers.*)

entender   ¿Entiende Ud. las palabras nuevas?
(*Sí, entiendo las palabras nuevas.*)
to understand   Do you understand the new words?
(*Yes, I understand the new words.*)

salir   ¿Sale Ud. del edificio?
(*Sí, salgo del edificio.*)
to leave (a place) Do you leave (from) the building?
(*Yes, I leave the building.*)

venir   ¿Viene Ud. temprano a misa?
(*Sí, vengo a misa temprano.*)
to come Do you come to Mass early?
(*Yes, I come to Mass early.*)

dormir   ¿Duerme Ud. ocho horas al día?
(*Sí, duermo ocho horas al día.*)
to sleep   Do you sleep 8 hours a day?
(*Yes, I sleep 8 hours a day.*)

volver   ¿Vuelve Ud. a casa ahora?
(*Sí, vuelvo a casa ahora.*)
to return   Are you returning home now?
(*Yes, I am returning home now.*)

recordar   ¿Recuerda Ud. la canción?
(*Sí, recuerdo la canción.*)
to remember   Do you remember the song?
(*Yes, I remember the song.*)

pedir   ¿Pide Ud. un favor?
(*Sí, pido un favor.*)
to ask (for)   Are you asking a favor?
(*Yes, I' am asking for a favor.*)

IR--to go (4-B)   (Listen and repeat)

(yo) VOY
Ud. VA ....   Juan VA....   Ella VA
(nosotros) VAMOS
Uds. VAN....Juan y Luis VAN... Ellas VAN
 ¿ADÓNDE va Ud?
--Voy a casa.
--Voy a misa.
--Voy a la casa de mi abuela.
--Voy al cine.   (4-C)
--Voy al restaurante.

I go
You go...Juan goes...She goes
We go
You (all) go...Juan and Luis go...They go
(to) Where are you going?
I'm going home.
I'm going to Mass.
I'm going to my grandmother's house.
I'm going to the movies.
I'm going to the restaurant.

(Substitute the new destination in the statement. The correct answer will follow.)

 ¿ADÓNDE va José?
--José va a la tienda. (a la iglesia)
--*José va a la iglesia.* (al templo)

Where is Jose going?
Jose goes to the store. (to the church)
Jose goes to the church. (to the temple)

Chapter 4 - A HAPPY OCCASION: THE NEW YEAR

--*José va al templo.* (a la sinagoga)   *Jose goes to the temple.* (to the synagogue)
--*José va a la sinagoga.* (al hospital)   *Jose goes to the synagogue.* (to the hospital)
--*José va al hospital.* (a las farmacias)   *Jose goes to the hospital.* (to the pharmacies)
--*José va a las farmacias.*   *Jose goes to the pharmacies.*

(Substitute the new time in the statement. The correct answer will follow.)

¿ Cuándo van ellos?   (a veces) (4-d)   When do they go? (at times)
--*Ellos van a veces.*   (muchas veces)   *They go at times.* (many times/often)
--*Ellos van muchas veces.*   (de vez en cuando)   *They go often.* (once in a while)
--*Ellos van de vez en cuando.*   (una vez al año)   *They go once in a while.* (once a month)
--*Ellos van una vez al año.*   (pocas veces)   *They go once a month.* (rarely)
--*Ellos van pocas veces.*   (con frecuencia)   *They go rarely.* (frequently)
--*Ellos van con frecuencia.*   (a las tres y media)   *They go frequently.* (at 3:30)
--*Ellos van a las tres y media.*   (cada octubre)   *They go at 3:30.* (each October)
--*Ellos van cada octubre.*   *They go each October.*
¿Cuándo van Uds.?   When are you (all) going?
--*Vamos la semana que viene.*   (mañana)   We go next week.(tomorrow)
--*Vamos mañana.*   (la próxima semana)   *We go tomorrow.* (next week)
--*Vamos la próxima semana.*   (el sábado)   *We go next week.* (on Saturday)
--*Vamos el sábado.*   *We go on Saturday.*

IR + a + INFINITIVE= going to do... (4-D)   (Listen and repeat)

Voy a enseñar la lección.   I am going to teach the lesson.
La monja va a rezar en la capilla.   The nun is going to pray in the chapel.
El sacerdote va a leer el evangelio.   The priest is going to read the Gospel.
La hermana no va a hacer nada.   The sister isn't going to do anything.
Vamos a hablar por teléfono.   We are going to speak on the phone.
El y yo no vamos a fumar aquí.   He and I are not going to smoke here.

THE FUTURE TENSE (4-E)

Voy a hablar---HABLARÉ   I am going to speak--I will speak
Voy a escribir--ESCRIBIRÉ   I am going to write--I will write
Voy a comer--COMERÉ   I am going to eat--I will eat
Ud va a hablar-- Ud. HABLARÁ   You are going to speak--You will speak
Ud. va a comer--Ud. COMERÁ   You are going to eat--You will eat
Vamos a hablar--HABLAREMOS   We are going to speak--We will speak

---

Chapter 4 - A HAPPY OCCASION: THE NEW YEAR

Vamos a comer--COMEREMOS
Uds. van a hablar--Uds. HABLARÁN
Uds. van a comer--Uds. COMERÁN
Voy a salir--SALDRÉ.
Ella va a salir--Ella SALDRÁ.
Voy a decir la verdad--DIRÉ la verdad.
Ellos van a decir la verdad--Ellos DIRÁN la verdad.
Voy a saber la respuesta--SABRÉ la respuesta.
Vamos a saber la respuesta--SABREMOS la respuesta.

We are going to eat--We will eat
You are going to speak--You will speak
You (pl.) are going to eat--You will eat
I am going to leave--I will leave.
She is going to leave--She will leave.
I am going to tell the truth--I will tell the truth.
They are going to say the truth--They will say the truth.
I am going to know the answer--I will know the answer.
We are going to know the answer--We will know the answer.

Me gustaría tomar --Tomaré (4-e)
Me gustaría amar al Señor--Amaré al Señor.
A ella no le gustaría robar--Ella no robará.
A él no le gustaría tener hambre --El no tendrá hambre.

I would like to take--I will take
I would like to love the Lord--I will love the Lord.
She wouldn't like to steal--She will not steal.
He wouldn't want to be hungry--He will not be hungry.

UNAS SELECCIONES DEL EVANGELIO

Jesús dijo--Yo soy el Pan de la Vida; él que a mí viene
 nunca tendrá hambre; y él que cree en mí, nunca tendrá sed.
         (Juan 6; 35)
El Gran Mandamiento que deben vivir todos los que creen
en Dios es:
"Amarás al Señor tu Dios con todo tu corazón, con toda
tu alma y con toda tu mente. Amarás a tu prójimo como
a ti mismo ."
   (Mateo 22; 37, 39)

SOME SELECTIONS FROM THE GOSPEL

Jesus said, "I am the bread of life; he who comes to me
will never be hungry; and he who believes in me will never
have thirst."
The great Commandment that all those who believe in God
is:
"You will love the Lord your God with all your heart, all your
your soul, with all your mind. You will love your neighbor
as yourself."

UNAS FRASES APROPIADAS PARA EL AÑO NUEVO

Les deseo a cada uno de Uds. un feliz Año Nuevo.

Recemos por la paz del mundo.

Que sea un Nuevo Año de esperanza y de riqueza espiritual.

Que la Virgen Madre le mantenga siempre en la paz de su Hijo.

Que el Señor les dé sabiduría y la gracia de su Hijo.

APPROPRIATE PHRASES FOR THE NEW YEAR

I wish each of you a Happy New Year.

Let us pray for peace in the world.

May the New Year be one of hope and spiritual richness.

May the Virgin grant each of you the peace of her Son.

May the Lord grant you wisdom and the grace of his Son.

GRAMMAR

4-A INDIRECT OBJECT PRONOUNS

a mí	ME	(to me)	a nosotros	NOS	(to us)
a ti	TE	(to you [familiar])			
a Ud.		(to you)	a Uds.		(to you [pl.])
a ella	LE	(to her)	a ellas	LES	(to them)
a él		(to him	a ellos		(to them)

GUSTARLE--to like   This phrase is important in any language, but because one is really saying **to someone it is pleasing,** this verb causes confusion for English speakers. The subject pronoun (*yo, Ud. ellos*) is NEVER used with the verb GUSTARLE. What would be a subject in English is the indirect object pronoun in Spanish.   Rather than trying to figure out why, it is probably easier to learn or memorize several examples.

(a mí) Me gusta el libro.   (a mí) Me gustan los libros. NOTE the use of the article (*el, los*) and the change from
(To me the book is pleasing.)   (To me the books are pleasing.)   GUSTA to GUSTAN when what is pleasing is plural.
(I like the book.)   (I like [the] books.)

A mí, a ti and *a nosotros* are usually omitted because it is obvious to whom they refer. Often in a conversation *¿le gusta?,* meaning *do you like it?* is enough. However, because *le* and *les* can refer to different people, it usually must be clarified with *a Ud., a Carlos, a ellos* along with the indirect object pronoun . Carefully study the examples below.

TO LIKE ONE THING

Me gusta el chocolate.   (I like chocolate.)
Te gusta el deporte.   (You like the sport.)
Nos gusta la flor.   (We like the flower.)

A Ud.   le gusta el coche.   (You like the car.)
A él   le gusta el coche.   (He likes the car.)
A Juan le gusta el coche.   (Juan likes the car.)
A ella   le gusta la silla.   (She likes the chair.)

A Uds.   les gusta la radio.   (You like the radio.)
A ellos   les gusta la fruta.   (They like fruit.)
A ellas   les gusta el anillo.   (They like the ring.)

TO LIKE SEVERAL THINGS

Me gustan los chocolates.   (I like chocolates.)
Te gustan los deportes.   (You like sports.)
Nos gustan las flores.   (We like [the] flowers.)

A Ud.   le gustan los coches. (You like cars.)
A él   le gustan los coches. (He likes [the] cars.)
A Juan le gustan los coches. (Juan likes [the] cars.)
A ella   le gustan las sillas.   (She likes [the] chairs.)

A Uds.   les gustan las radios. (You like the radios.)
A ellos   les gustan las frutas. (They like fruits.)
A ellas   les gustan los anillos. (They like [the] rings.)

GUSTARLE never takes a direct object pronoun. If one wants to say *I like it* or *I like them* one simply uses the shorter form:

Me gusta. (I like it.)   Me gustan. (I like them.)
A Juan le gusta. (Juan likes it.)   A Juan le gustan. (Juan likes them.)

GUSTARLE + the infinitive= *to like to do something.*

Me gusta leer.   (I like to read or I like reading.)
Nos gusta conversar.   (We like to converse.)
A Ud. le gusta dormir.   (You like to sleep.)
A ellos les gusta trabajar. (They like to work.)

ME GUSTARÍA= *I would like* (The conditional tense is introduced here but explained in Chapter 10.)

Me gustaría un chocolate.   (I would like a chocolate.)
Me gustarían unos chocolates.   (I would like some chocolates.)
Me gustaría escuchar las cintas. (I would like to listen to the tapes.)

The placement of the indirect object pronoun is different in Spanish. As with GUSTARLE, the pronoun goes BEFORE the verb:

Carlos me da el libro. (Carlos gives the book to me or Carlos gives me the book.)
Yo le doy el libro a Carlos. (I give the book to him or I give him the book.)

With an infinitive or a gerund (see Chapters 7 and 11) the object pronoun is attached to the infinitive or gerund or is separate and before the infinitive or gerund.

1) Carlos quiere darme el regalo.   (Carlos wants to give me the gift.)
    Carlos está dándome el regalo.   (Carlos is giving me the gift.)

2) Carlos me quiere dar el regalo.   (Carlos wants to give me the gift.)
    Carlos me está dando el regalo.   (Carlos is giving me the gift.)

4-B IR--to go

yo	voy		
tú	vas		
Ud.	va		
nosotros	vamos		
Uds.	van		

As in English, one goes *to* a place. ¿ ADÓNDE va Carlos?   (TO WHERE is Carlos going?)

Carlos va a la tienda.   (Carlos goes to the store.)
Carlos va a las tiendas.   (Carlos goes to the stores.)
Carlos va al restaurante.   (Carlos goes to the restaurant.) [4-C]
Carlos va a los hospitales. (Carlos goes to the hospitals.)

4-C CONTRACTIONS

a + el = **al**   a + el señor = **al** señor   (to the man)
             a + el restaurante = al restaurante (to the restaurant)

de + el = **del**   de + el señor = del señor (of the man)
             de + el restaurante = del restaurante (of the restaurant)

4-D   IR + A + Infinitive = *going to do something*

Voy a visitar a mi abuela.   (I am going to visit my grandmother.)
Carmen va a leer.   (Carmen is going to read.)
Ellos van a comer en el restaurante mexicano. (They are going to eat in the Mexican restaurante.)

4-E   THE FUTURE TENSE

One group of personal endings is added to the entire infinitive:

	HABLAR	COMER	VIVIR	
yo	hablaré	comeré	viviré	(I will speak, eat, live)
tú	hablarás	comerás	vivirás	(You [fam.] will speak, eat, live)
Ud.	hablará	comerá	vivirá	(You will speak, eat, live)
nosotros	hablaremos	comeremos	viviremos	(We will speak, eat, live)
Uds.	hablarán	comerán	vivirán	(You [pl.] will speak, eat, live)

The more common irregular verbs in the future tense are:

DECIR (to say)   diré, dirás, dirá, diremos, dirán
HACER (to make, do) haré, harás, hará, haremos, harán
QUERER (to want)   querré, querrás, querrá, querremos, querrán
SABER (to know)   sabré, sabrás, sabrá, sabremos, sabrán
SALIR   (to leave)   saldré, saldrás, saldrá, saldremos, saldrán
TENER (to have)   tendré, tendrás, tendrá, tendremos, tendrán
PODER (to be able)   podré, podrás, podrá, podremos, podrán
VENIR (to come)   vendré, vendrás, vendrá, vendremos, vendrán
PONER (to put)   pondré, pondrás, pondrá, pondremos, pondrán

PRESENT TENSE IRREGULAR VERBS INTRODUCED IN THIS CHAPTER:

	DAR--to give	DECIR--to say	HACER-to make	SALIR-to leave	VENIR-to come
yo	doy	digo	hago	salgo	vengo
tú	das	dices	haces	sales	vienes
Ud.	da	dice	hace	sale	viene
nosotros	damos	decimos	hacemos	salimos	venimos
Uds.	dan	dicen	hacen	salen	vienen

In the present tense there are quite a few STEM-CHANGING VERBS, some of which are regular in other tenses.
Such verbs follow the--AR , --ER or --IR endings, but the there is a stem change E > IE or O > UE in all persons except *nosotros*.

	RECORDER--to remember	VOLVER--to return	DORMIR--to sleep	ENTENDER-to understand
yo	recuerdo	vuelvo	duermo	entiendo
tú	recuerdas	vuelves	duermes	entiendes
Ud.	recuerda	vuelve	duerme	entiende
nosotros	recordamos	volvemos	dormimos	entendemos
Uds.	recuerdan	vuelven	duermen	entienden

One group of verbs change from E > I   (PEDIR-to ask for, SERVIR-to serve, REPETIR-to repeat)

PEDIR-to ask (for)

yo	pido
tú	pides
Ud.	pide
nosotros	pedimos
Uds.	piden

VOCABULARY AND CULTURAL NOTES

a) *jugar al fútbol*--to play soccer (*fútbol americano* = football) In standard Spanish *a* is used after the verb JUGAR before sports or games. Since most sports are masculine in Spanish, this usually becomes *jugar al*. Some examples are:

Ellos van a jugar al tenis. (They are going to play tennis.) Jugaré al béisbol. (I will play baseball.)

TOCAR--to play a musical instrument or touch something. An example is: Ud. toca el piano. (You play the piano.)

b) *la lección---las lecciones* (the lesson, the lessons) All words in Spanish that end in --CIÓN or --SIÓN are feminine and carry a written accent on the letter *o* in the singular. However, the written accent is always dropped from these words in the plural.

canción---canciones (song, songs), selección---selecciones (selection, selections), procesión---procesiones (procession, processions), conversación---conversaciones (conversation, conversations), acción---acciones (action, actions).

c) *escuchar* (listen to) Several verbs in Spanish do not need a preposition as they do in English. *Escuchar la música* means *to listen TO music*. Other common verbs that include the proposition are: ESPERAR (to hope or to wait FOR); BUSCAR (to look FOR); PAGAR (to pay FOR); PEDIR (to ask FOR).

d) *a veces* (sometimes, at times) The word *time* translates into several words in Spanish. *¿Qué hora es?* (What time is it?) refers to clock (hour) time. *Vez*, plural *veces*, is used in adverbial phrases such as *la primera vez* (the first time), *muchas veces* (many times, often), *pocas veces* (few times, seldom), *de vez en cuando* (once in a while), *una vez al año* (once a year), *la próxima vez* (next time), *la última vez* (the last time). *Tiempo* also means *time* as in *No tengo tiempo.* (I don't have time.)
Note that *tiempo* when used with the verb HACER refers to weather. *¿Qué tiempo hace?--Hace buen tiempo.* (What is the weather like?--It is nice.)

e) The verb TOMAR means *to get a cab or train, to take, even to eat or drink*. This most versatile of verbs often can substitute for the verb COGER, which means *to get, take or pick* in Spain and the Caribbean, but means *f---k* in Mexico, Argentina and several other countries. The second verb will not be used in this text. Words change meaning in different regions and time periods but that verb may be the most dramatic. It is frustrating when sometimes an acceptable word in one place takes another meaning in another country or among a different social group. On the bright side, it indicates the richness and flexibilty of the language.

CHAPTER 5

A SAD OCCASION: SICKNESS AND DEATH

TAPESCRIPT

SER---descripción general (5-A)

(repetición)

¿Cómo es la iglesia?
La iglesia es bonita.
Las flores son blancas.
Mi abuelo es generoso.
La hermana Cecilia es simpática.
Los nietos son agradables.
Pedro es un hombre sincero.
Pedro es una persona sincera. (5-a)
Cecilia es una mujer honesta.
Cecilia es una persona honesta.
Pedro es una víctima inocente.
Cecilia es una víctima inocente.

Ana es soltera.
Su madre es casada.
La abuela de Ana es viuda.
El señor Gómez es viudo.

TO BE--general description

(repetition).

What does the church look like?
The church is pretty.
The flowers are white.
My grandfather is generous.
Sister Cecilia is nice.
The grandchildren are nice.
Pedro is a sincere man.
Pedro is a sincere person.
Cecilia is an honest woman.
Cecilia is an honest person.
Pedro is an innocent victim.
Cecilia is an innocent victim.

Ana is single (unmarried).
Her mother is married.
Ana's grandmother is a widow.
Mr. Gomez is a widower.

¿Cómo es Mario?
--Mario es alto y guapo.
¿Cómo es Adelita?
--Adelita es alta y guapa.

What does Mario look like?
Mario is tall and handsome.
What does Adelita look like?
Adelita is tall and pretty.

SER--la profesión o el trabajo

TO BE--profession or work

el empleo
el desempleo
Necesito empleo. (trabajo)
el empleado---la empleada
el obrero---la obrera
el peón
el carpintero---la carpintera
el dependiente---la dependienta
el abogado---la abogada
el juez---la juez
el mecánico---la mecánica (la mecánico)
el oficinista---la oficinista
el organista---la organista
la monja (la hermana católica)
el cura o el sacerdote (el pastor)

employment
unemployment
I need employment. (work)
employee (male and female)
worker (laborer)
farm worker
carpenter (male and female)
salesperson (male and female)
lawyer (male and female)
judge (male and female)
mechanic (male and female) (*female mechanic* in some countries)
office worker (male and female)
organist (male and female)
nun
priest (pastor--literally *shepherd*)

Soy pastor de una parroquia hispana.
Paco es mecánico.
Nuestro hijo es oficinista.
Ana es organista.
Ana es dependienta.
Ellas son monjas.
Dios es nuestro juez.

I am the pastor of an Hispanic parish.
Paco is a mechanic.
Our son is an office worker.
Ana is an organist.
Ana is a salesperson.
They are nuns.
God is our judge.

SER--el país de origen y nacionalidad

TO BE-- country of origin and nationality

Raúl es de Cuba; él es cubano.
Javier es del Perú; él es peruano.
Carolina es de México; ella es mexicana.
Soy de Puerto Rico; soy puertorriqueña.
Ellos son de España; son españoles.

Raul is from Cuba; he is Cuban.
Xavier is from Peru; he is Peruvian.
Caroline is from Mexico; she is Mexican.
I am from Puerto Rico; I'm Puerto Rican.
They are from Spain; they are Spanish.

Chapter 5 - A SAD OCCASION: SICKNESS AND DEATH

¿De dónde es Pepe?   Where is Pepe from?
--Pepe es de El Salvador.   Pepe is from El Salvador.
¿Es dominicano su papá?   Is your father Dominican?
--No, mi papá no es dominicano.   No, my father is not Dominican.
Mi papá es colombiano.   My father is Colombian.

ESTAR--to be --with health and location   (5-B)

¿Cómo ESTÁ Mario?   How is Mario (his health)?
--Mario está bien.   Mario is well (fine).
--Mario está enfermo.   Mario is sick.
--Mario está cansado.   (5-b)   Mario is tired.
--Mario está deprimido.   Mario is depressed.
¿Cómo se siente Mario?   How does Mario feel?
--Mario no se siente bien.   Mario doesn't feel well.
--Mario no está bien.   Mario isn't well.
--Mario se siente mejor.   Mario feels better.
¿Cómo está Ana?   How is Ana?
¿Cómo se siente Ana?   How does Ana feel?
--Ana está bien.   Ana is well.
--Ana está enferma.   Ana is sick.
--Ana se siente enferma.   Ana feels sick.
--Ana está cansada.   Ana is tired.
--Ana está deprimida   Ana is depressed.

¿DÓNDE ESTÁ MARIO?   Where is Mario?
Mario ESTÁ EN el hospital.   Mario is in the hospital.
             casa.   at home.
             la oficina.   the office.
¿Dónde está Ud?   Where are you?
--ESTOY EN la fábrica (factoría).   I'm in the factory.
             la rectoría.   the rectory.

ESTAR---frases especiales   TO BE---special phrases

Mario está enfermo.   Mario is sick.
Mario está triste.   Mario is sad.
Mario está contento.   Mario is happy.
Mario está preocupado.   Mario is worried.

Ana está preocupada por su hijo.	Ana is worried about her son.
Mario está ocupado.	Mario is busy.
Ana está ocupada con su trabajo.	Ana is busy with her job.
Mario está enojado (enfadado).	Mario is angry.
Ana no está enojada (enfadada).	Ana isn't angry.

UNAS DIFERENCIAS : SER + ESTAR / SOME DIFFERENCES : SER + ESTAR

Mario ES débil.	Mario is weak.
Mario ESTÁ débil.	Mario seems or looks weak.
Mario ES gordo.	Mario is fat.
Mario ESTÁ gordo.	Mario looks fat.
Ana ES bonita.	Ana is pretty.
Ana ESTÁ bonita.	Ana looks pretty (is all dressed up).
Ana ES borracha.	Ana is a drunk (an alcoholic).
Ana ESTÁ borracha.	Ana is drunk (but not habitually).

TENER--modismos especiales (1-d) / TO HAVE--special idioms

(yo) TENGO Pepe tiene	I have Pepe has
Tengo treinta años.	I am 30 years old.
Tengo frío.	I am cold.
Cuando tengo frío, necesito un suéter.	When I am cold I need a sweater.
Tengo calor.	I am hot.
Cuando tengo calor, quiero un refresco.	When I am hot I want a soft drink.
Tengo hambre.	I am hungry.
el hombre	the man (watch the pronunciation!)
Tengo mucha hambre.	I am very hungry.
El hombre tiene hambre.	The man is hungry.
Cuando tengo hambre, quiero comer.	When I am hungry I want to eat.
Tengo sed.	I am thirsty.
Cuando tengo sed, quiero beber algo.	When I am thirsty I want to drink something.
Pepe tiene miedo.	Pepe is afraid.
Pepe tiene miedo de la muerte.	Pepe is afraid of death.
de los perros.	of dogs.
de su padre.	of his father.
Tenemos sueño.	We are sleepy.
Tenemos sueño y queremos dormir.	We are sleepy and want to sleep.
Estamos cansados.	We are tired.

Estamos cansados y queremos descansar.	We are tired and want to rest.
Ana tiene suerte.	Ana is lucky.
No tengo suerte; tengo mala pata.	I am unlucky. (literally, *a bad paw*)
¡Buena suerte!	Good luck!
¡Le espero mucha suerte!	I wish you much luck!

(Answer the questions with the provided information. The correct answer will follow.)

¿Cómo está Marta? (enferma)	How is Marta? (sick)
--*Marta está enferma.*	*Marta is sick.*
¿Cómo está Pepe? (cansado)	How is Pepe? (tired)
--*Pepe está cansado.*	*Pepe is tired.*
¿Cómo es Carlos? (alto y amable)	What is Carlos like? (tall and nice)
--*Carlos es alto y amable.*	*Carlos is tall and nice.*
¿Cómo está su madre hoy? (deprimida)	How is your mother today? (depressed)
--*Mi madre está deprimida hoy.*	*My mother is depressed today.*
¿Cómo se siente su abuelo? (mejor)	How does your grandfather feel? (better)
--*Mi abuelo se siente mejor.*	*My grandfather feels better.*
¿Está enojado el padrino? (sí)	Is the godfather angry? (yes)
--*Sí, el padrino está enojado.*	*Yes, the godfather is angry.*
¿Está débil la viuda? (sí)	Does the widow seem weak? (yes)
--*Sí, la viuda está débil.*	*Yes, the widow seems weak.*
¿Está contento o triste el niño? (triste)	Is the boy happy or sad? (sad)
--*El niño está triste.*	*The boy is sad.*
¿Tiene Ud frío o calor ? (frío)	Are you cold or hot? (cold)
--*Tengo frío.*	*I am cold.*
¿Tiene Ud hambre o sed? (hambre)	Are you hungry or thirsty? (hungry)
--*Tengo hambre.*	*I am hungry.*
Si Ud está cansado, ¿qué quiere hacer? (descansar)	If you are tired, what do you want to do? (rest)
--*Si estoy cansado quiero descansar.*	*If I am tired I want to rest.*
Si ella tiene sueño, ¿qué quiere hacer? (dormir)	If she is tired, what does she want to do? (sleep)
--*Si ella tiene sueño, quiere dormir.*	*If she is sleepy, she wants to sleep.*

DEMONSTRATIVE ADJECTIVES (5-C)

(Listen and repeat)

este libro	this book
estos libros	these books

esta familia---aquí (acá)	this family---here
estas familias--aquí (acá)	these families---here
esta estudiante	this (female) student
este estudiante	this (male) student
estas pacientes	these (female) patients
estos pacientes	these (male) patients
ese libro	that book
esos libros---ahí	those books---there (nearby)
esa familia cubana	that Cuban family
esas familias mexicanas	those Mexican families
ese pariente	that relative (male)
esos parientes	those relatives
esa parienta	that relative (female)
esas parientas	those relatives (female only)
Esta situación es difícil.	This situation is difficult.
Este trabajo es complicado.	This work is complicated.
Estos carpinteros son buenos.	These carpenters are good.
Esos carpinteros son malos.	Those carpenters are bad.
Esa iglesia es moderna.	That church is modern.
este libro---ese libro	this book---that book
esta palabra---esa palabra	this word---that word
este libro--aquí (acá)	this book--here
ese libro---ahí	that book --there (nearby)
aquel libro---allí (allá)	that book--far off (in time or space)
aquella casa---aquellas casas	that house---those houses
Tengo buenas memorias de	I have good memories of
aquellos tiempos.	those (good old) times.
aquella época.	that (long ago) period.

UNEQUAL COMPARISONS (5-D)

El libro es interesante.	The book is interesting.
El libro es MÁS interesante.	The book is more interesting.
La casa es bonita.	The house is pretty.
La casa es MÁS bonita.	The house is prettier. (more pretty)
Las casas son más bonitas.	The houses are prettier.

El estudiante es guapo.
El estudiante es MENOS guapo.
La estudiante es menos guapa.

The student is handsome.
The student is less handsome.
The (female) student is less pretty.

Este libro es más interesante.
Ese libro es menos interesante.
Este libro es MÁS interesante QUE ese libro.

This book is more interesting.
That book is less interesting.
This book is more interesting than that book.

Esta flor es más linda.
Esa flor es menos linda.
Esta flor es más linda que esa flor.
Esa flor es menos linda que esta flor.
Soy más alto que mi hermano.
Mi hermano es menos alto que yo.
Mi hermano es más bajo que yo.
Estas cintas son más difíciles que esas cintas.

This flower is prettier
That flower is less pretty
This flower is prettier than that flower
That flower is less pretty than this flower
I am taller than my brother
My brother is less tall (shorter) than I am
My brother is shorter than I am
These tapes are more difficult than those tapes.

Esas casas son menos viejas que
    aquellas casas.

Those houses are less old than
    those houses (far away).

SOME IRREGULAR COMPARISONS

bueno----MEJOR
malo-----PEOR
grande--más grande o MAYOR
pequeño--más pequeño o MENOR

good-----better
bad----worse
big--bigger (age or size)
small---smaller (age or size)

Este libro es bueno pero ese libro es mejor.
Mi abuela está mejor.
El paciente se siente peor.
Estas lecciones son malas pero
    esas lecciones eran peores.
Mi hermana mayor
El altar mayor
Soy mayor que mi amigo.
(Tengo más años que mi amigo.)
Mi hermana menor

This book is good but that book es mejor.
My grandmother is better.
The patient feels worse.
These lessons are bad but
    those lessons were worse.
My older (bigger) sister
The main (larger) altar
I'm older than my friend.
I'm older than my friend.
My younger (smaller) sister

SUPERLATIVES

Juan es EL MÁS alto.	Juan is the tallest.
Juanita es LA MÁS baja.	Juanita is the shortest.
Juanita es LA MENOS alta.	Juanita is the least tall.
Somos LOS MÁS inteligentes.	We are the smartest.
Juan es EL MÁS alto DE la clase.	Juan is the tallest IN the class.
Juanita es LA MEJOR DE la clase.	Juanita is the best IN the class.
Juan es EL PEOR DE la clase.	Juan is the worst IN the class.
Rosario es la mujer más guapa del mundo.	Rosario is the most beautiful woman in the world.

LA ENFERMEDAD Y LA MUERTE / ILLNESS AND DEATH

(Repetición) / (Repetition)

la enfermedad	illness, sickness
el enfermo, la enferma	the sick person
la enfermera, el enfermero	nurse
La enfermera cuida a la paciente.	The nurse cares for the patient.
La enfermera ayuda al paciente.	The nurse helps the male patient.
el sufrimiento	the suffering
sufrir (padecer)	to suffer
Carlos sufre del cáncer.	Carlos suffers from cancer.
Mi tía sufre del corazón.	My aunt suffers from heart problems.
(yo) Sufro del hígado.	I suffer from liver problems.
El paciente padece de una enfermedad.	The patient suffers from an illness.
Cristo sufrió por nosotros.	Christ suffered for us.
el dolor---los dolores	pain, sorrow
Carlos no tiene mucho dolor.	Carlos doesn't have much pain.
Nuestra Señora de los Dolores	Our Lady of Sorrows
la operación	the operation
Lo (la) operaron ayer.	They operated on him (her) yesterday.
La situación es grave.	The situation is grave (serious).
Dicen que el enfermo va a morir.	They say the sick man is going to die.
el moribundo (la moribunda)	the dying man (woman)
El enfermo quiere confesar.	The sick man wants to confess.
La enferma quiere el sacramento.	The sick woman wants the sacrament.
No siempre comprendemos la voluntad de Dios.	We do not always understand the will of God.
misericordia	mercy

Dios ofrece misericordia.	God offers mercy.
compasión.	compassion.
consuelo.	comfort.
El señor murió de un ataque al corazón.	The man died of a heart attack.
Tengo que visitar a la viuda.	I must visit the widow.
Tengo que consolar a la familia.	I must console the family.
Hay que planear el velorio.	One must plan the wake.
el funeral.	the funeral.
el entierro.	the burial.

DIÁLOGO PARA ARREGLAR UN FUNERAL

FUNERAL ARRANGEMENTS

SEÑORA--Murió mi padre hace unas horas
en el hospital. Le dieron el sacramento de los
enfermos anoche. Eso me consuela un poco.

My father died a few hours ago
in the hospital. They gave him the sacrament
of the sick last night. That consoles me a bit.

PADRE--¡Cuánto lo siento!

I'm so sorry!

SEÑORA--Pues, mi hermano va a arreglar
el velorio para mañana en la Funeraria Paz.
Quiero arreglar la misa fúnebre con Ud.
Mi madre no está en condiciones...
¿Es posible tener la misa el jueves por
la mañana, tal vez a las diez?

Well, my brother is going to arrange the wake
for tomorrow in Paz Funeral Home. I want
arrange the funeral mass with you.
My mother is in no condition...
Is it possible to have the mass on Thursday
morning, perhaps at 10:00?

PADRE---Está libre la iglesia a esa hora.
No hay inconveniente.

The church is free at that hour.
There is no problem.

SEÑORA--Estoy tan deprimida. Todo
parece imposible...Pero, después de todo
papá tenía setenta años y estaba débil.
Ud. sabe que él padecía del corazón.
Ud. lo visitó después de la operación.

I am so depressed. It all seems
impossible...But, after all
Papa was 70 and he was weak (ill).
You know that he suffered from heart problems.
You visited him after the operation.

PADRE--La muerte siempre nos sorprende.
No siempre comprendemos la voluntad
de Dios. Su padre era un buen hombre y
ahora está en paz con Dios.

Death always surprises us.
We do not always understand the will
of God. Your father was a good man and
is at peace with God.

Que la fe la fortalezca a Ud.

May your faith keep you strong.

SEÑORA--Gracias, Padre. La
funeraria se hace cargo de la carroza
fúnebre y mi hermano organiza a los
seis portadores de féretro. Queremos
la organista.

Thanks, Father. The funeral home
takes care of the hearse
and my brother is taking care of the
six pallbearers. We want the organist.

PADRE-- ¿Alguna música especial o selección
del Evangelio o del Antiguo Testamento?

Any special music or selection
from the Gospel or the Old Testament?

SEÑORA--Tal vez el Salmo 23.
Le gustaba. Ud. puede escoger
Ud. conocía bien a Papá. Todo
digno pero simple. El entierro
es en el cementerio Calvary.
Tengo que volver a casa y llamar
a más parientes. Vuelvo aquí a la
una y podemos terminar los detalles.
Bendición, padre.

Maybe the 23rd Psalm. He used to like it.
You can chose.
You knew Papa well. Everything
dignified but simple. The burial
is in Calvary cementery.
I must return home and call more
relatives. I'll return here at 1:00
and we can finish the details.
A blessing, Father.

PADRE--Que Dios te bendiga,
te llene de la luz y fuerza que
es su presencia. Que Dios te ampare
y consuele en este momento de dolor.

May God bless you,
may you be filled with the light and power
of His presence. May God help and
and console you in this moment of sorrow.

GRAMMAR

5-A   USES OF SER --TO BE   GENERAL DESCRIPTION: color, size, material

SER   NOUNS AND ADJECTIVES USED WITH *SER* MUST AGREE IN NUMBER AND GENDER

	SER	
yo	soy	¿Cómo es Carlos? (What does Carlos look like?)
tú	eres	--Carlos es alto. (Carlos is tall.)
Ud.	es	Elena y su prima son bonitas. (Elena and her cousin are pretty.)
nosotros	somos	El anillo es de oro. (The ring is of gold.)
Uds.	son	La casa es blanca pero vieja. (The house is white but old.)

NATIONAL ORIGIN AND NATIONALITY

María Luisa es de Cuba.   María Luisa es cubana.
(Maria Luisa is from Cuba.)   (Maria Luisa is Cuban.)   NOTE: Nationalities are not capitalized in Spanish.

Argentina-----argentino/a   Bolivia-----boliviano/a   Costa Rica-----costarricense
Colombia-----colombiano/a   Cuba--------cubano/a   Nicaragua-----nicaragüense
Chile----------chileno/a   Ecuador----ecuatoriano/a   los Estados Unidos--(norte)americano/a
México-------mexicano/a   El Salvador-salvadoreño/a
Guatemala---guatemalteco/a   Honduras---hondureño/a   Somos (norte)americanos. Somos de Nueva York.
Panamá------panameño/a   Paraguay---paraguayo/a   (We are American. We are from New York.)
Perú---------peruano/a   Uruguay----uruguayo/a   Teresa es costarricense y su esposo es nicaragüense.
Venezuela--venezolano/a   Puerto Rico-puertorriqueño/a   (Teresa is Costa Rican and her husband is Nicaraguan.)
República Dominicana--dominicano/a   España--español/ española

SER WITH PROFESSION OR WORK

Most jobs and professions are listed in the dictionary in the masculine form but by a simple change can be made feminine

el carpintero   (male carpenter)   la carpintera (female carpenter)

With some words only the article indicates the gender: el estudiante (male student)   la estudiante (female student)

Words that end in --ISTA only change the article: el oficinista (male office worker) la oficinista (female office worker)
pesimista (pessimist), optimista (optimist), dentista (dentist), turista (tourist), comunista (communist) are other examples.

5-B   ESTAR   HEALTH AND LOCATION

yo	estoy
tú	estás
Ud.	está
nosotros	estamos
Uds.	están

¿ Cómo está Ud?   (How are you?)
--Estoy enfermo.   (I am sick)
¿ Dónde está la enfermera? (Where is the nurse?)

ESTAR WITH SPECIAL PHRASES: happy, sad, depressed, angry, drunk, worried

La viuda está triste y deprimida.   (The widow is sad and depressed.)
Los niños están contentos con los regalos. (The children are happy with the gifts.)

ESTAR MEANING *LOOKS* OR *SEEMS*

Elena está muy bonita en ese vestido nuevo. (Elena *looks* pretty in that new dress.)
Alfonso está débil después de la operación.   (Alsonso *seems* weak after the operation.)

TENER with special phrases (see Chapter 1) may translate as *is*, as in *Tengo hambre*. Literally this is *I have hunger* although it sounds better in English as *I am hungry*. *Hambre* functions as a noun, not as an adjective.

5-C   DEMONSTRATIVE ADJECTIVES

AQUI / /ACA (HERE)   AHÍ (THERE)   ALLÍ // ALLÁ (THERE far away in time or space)

este libro	(this book)	ese libro	(that book)	aquel libro	(that book)
estos libros	(these books)	esos libros	(those books)	aquellos libros	(those books)
esta silla	(this chair)	esa silla	(that chair)	aquella silla	(that chair)
estas sillas	(these chairs)	esas sillas	(those chairs)	aquellas sillas	(those chairs)

5-D   UNEQUAL COMPARISONS

MÁS + adjective /noun	más bonita (prettier)	más alto (taller)	más dinero (more money)
MÁS + adjective + QUE	más bonita que (prettier than)	más alto que (taller than)	
MÁS + noun + QUE	más dinero que (more money than)	más libros que (more books than)	
MENOS + adjective/ noun	menos bonita (less pretty)	menos alto (less tall)	menos dinero (less money)
MENOS + adjective/noun + QUE	menos bonita que (less pretty than)	menos dinero que (less money than)	

IRREGULAR COMPARISONS

bueno---MEJOR (good--better)   malo---PEOR (bad---worse)
grande--más grande // MAYOR   (big--bigger or older)
pequeño--más pequeño// MENOR   (smaller--smaller or younger)

SUPERLATIVES

article + (noun) + MÁS/ MENOS + adjective
 el   niño   más   alto   (the tallest boy)
 la   más   linda   (the prettiest)
 los   niños   menos   gordos   (the least fat children)

Carlos es el (niño) más alto DE la clase.   (Carlos is the tallest [boy] IN the class.)

VOCABULARY AND CULTURAL NOTES

a) Several words can apply to men or women without the usual gender accommodations. *Una persona* and *una víctima* are such words.

Juan es una buena persona. (Juan is a good person.)   Olga es una buena persona. (Olga is a good person.)

b) In every language there are words with very different meanings with only a letter difference. One must take special care to keep the meanings straight. Two such examples appear in this chapter: CANSADO (tired)---CASADO (married) and HOMBRE (man)--HAMBRE (hunger). Other such confusions are: PECADO (sin) --- PESCADO (fish) and OVEJA (sheep)---OREJA (ear). Hispanic parishioners are generally pleased when others try to speak Spanish. They may smile at small errors but usually only correct you if you say something really strange or if you ask to be corrected. Even when you mispronounce a word, many Spanish-speakers will be able to guess what you mean to say and will help you along.

CHAPTER 6

ASH WEDNESDAY AND LENT

TAPESCRIPT

SOME PHRASES THAT USE INFINITIVES

(Listen and repeat)

Necesito trabajar.	I need to work.
Quiero trabajar.	I want to work.
Voy a trabajar.	I am going to work.
Me gusta trabajar.	I like to work.
Puedo trabajar.	I can (am able) to work.
Sé trabajar.	I know how to work.
Prefiero trabajar.	I prefer to work.
Hágame el FAVOR DE trabajar.	Do me the favor of working.
FAVOR DE trabajar. (6-A)	Please work (shortened form of above).

THE PRESENT TENSE AND COMMANDS

(Listen and repeat)

(trabajar) (yo) trabajo Ud. trabaja	(to work) I work you work
TRABAJE Ud., por favor.	Work, please.
Favor de trabajar.	Please work.
(comprar) (yo) compro Ud. compra	(to buy) I buy You buy
COMPRE Ud. un regalo.	Buy a gift.

Favor de comprar un regalo.	Please buy a gift.
(usar) (yo) uso Ud. usa	(to use) I use You use
USE Ud. el diccionario.	Use the dicctionary.
Favor de usar el diccionario.	Please use the dictionary.
(dejar) (yo) dejo Ud. deja	(to leave-an item) I leave You leave
DEJE Ud. su vieja vida.	Leave your old life.
(hablar) (yo) hablo Ud. habla	(to speak) I speak You speak
HABLE Ud. por teléfono.	Speak on the phone.
Favor de hablar por teléfono.	Please speak on the phone.
(regresar) (yo) regreso Ud. regresa	(to return) I return You return
REGRESE Ud. a Cristo.	Return to Christ.
(comenzar) (yo) comienzo Ud. comienza	(to begin) I begin You begin
COMIENCE Ud. una nueva vida.	Begin a new life.
Favor de comenzar una nueva vida.	Please begin a new life.
(pensar) (Yo) pienso Ud. piensa	(to think) I think You think
Pienso que es importante.	I think that it is important.
Pienso en mi familia. (6-a)	I think about my family.
PIENSE Ud. en el Señor.	Think about the Lord.
(comer) (yo) como Ud. come	(to eat) I eat You eat
COMA Ud. el helado.	Eat the ice cream.
Favor de comer el helado.	Please eat the ice cream.
(recibir) (yo) recibo Ud. recibe	(to receive) I receive You receive
RECIBA Ud. la cenizas.	Receive the ashes.
Favor de recibir las cenizas.	Please receive the ashes.
(leer) (yo) leo Ud. lee	(to read) I read You read
LEA Ud. el evangelio.	Read the Gospel.
Favor de leer el evangelio.	Please read the Gospel.
(creer) (yo) creo Ud. cree	(to believe) I believe You believe
CREA Ud. en el amor de Dios.	Believe in the love of God.
Favor de creer en el amor de Dios.	Please believe in the love of God.
Favor de practicar obras de caridad.	Please practice charitable works.
(yo) practico Ud. practica	I practice You practice
PRACTIQUE Ud.	Practice (you singular)
PRACTIQUEN Uds.	Practice (you plural)
Favor de llegar a tiempo.	Please arrive on time.
(yo) llego Ud. llega	I arrive You arrive
LLEGUE Ud. a tiempo.	Arrive on time.
LLEGUEN Uds. a tiempo.	Arrive (you plural) on time.

(In the following exercises you will be asked to provide the plural form of the command)

(yo) tengo -- TENGA Ud.
(TENGAN Uds.)
(yo) digo--- DIGA Ud.
(DIGAN Uds.)
(yo) conozco ---CONOZCA Ud. a Carlos
(CONOZCAN Uds. a Carlos)
(yo) voy---VAYA Ud. a casa.
(VAYAN Uds. a casa)
(yo) salgo---SALGA Ud. de mi oficina.
(SALGAN Uds. de mi oficina.)
(yo) vuelvo ----VUELVA Ud. a Cristo.
(VUELVAN Uds. a Cristo.)
(yo) hago ---HAGA Ud. el trabajo.
(HAGAN Uds. el trabajo.)
(yo) soy ---SEA Ud. un buen cristiano. (6-b)
(SEAN Uds. unos buenos cristianos)
(yo) doy ----DÉ Ud. un regalo.
(DÉN Uds. un regalo.)
(yo) estoy ----ESTÉ Ud. siempre con nosotros.
(ESTÉN Uds. siempre con nosotros.)
(yo) vengo----VENGA Ud. a la rectoría.
(VENGAN Uds. a la rectoría.)

I have---have
(Have--you plural)
I say--- say
(Say)
I know---Know Carlos
(Know Carlos)
I go---Go home.
(Go home.)
I leave---Leave my office.
(Leave my office.)
I return---Return to Christ.
(Return to Christ.)
I do (make) ---Do the work.
(Do the work.)
I am---Be a good Christian.
(Be good Christians)
I give---Give a gift.
(Give a gift.)
I am---Always be with us.
(Always be with us.)
I come---Come to the rectory.
(Come to the rectory.)

UN PEQUEÑO DESCANSO DE LOS VERBOS

(Escuche y repita Ud.)

¿Qué es *Cuaresma?*
¿Qué significa *Cuaresma?*
¿Qué quiere decir *Cuaresma?*
Significa...
Quiere decir...
La palabra *Cuaresma* quiere decir cuarenta días.
Son los cuarenta días de ayuno que hizo Jesús.
Representa los cuarenta años de los israelitas en el desierto.
¿Comprende Ud.? --Sí, comprendo.
¿Entiende Ud.? --Sí, entiendo.

A SHORT BREAK FROM VERBS

(Listen and repeat)

What is *Cuaresma?*
What does Lent mean?
What does Lent mean?
It means (signifies)...
It means...
The word Lent means 40 days.
They are the 40 days of fasting that Jesus did.
It represents the 40 years of the Israelites in the desert.
Do you understand? --Yes, I understand.
Do you understand? -- Yes, I understand.

¿Comprende Ud. el significado?--Sí, comprendo. | Do you understand the meaning? Yes, I understand.
Tiene sentido. | It makes sense.
No tiene mucho sentido. | It doesn't make much sense.
La Cuaresma comienza el Miércoles de Ceniza. | Lent begins on Ash Wednesday.

THE SUBJUNCTIVE: DIRECT AND INDIRECT COMMANDS

(Listen and repeat)

(hablar) HABLE Ud. en voz baja. | (to speak) Speak in a whisper (low voice).
Que Ud. HABLE en voz baja. (6-B) | May you speak in a whisper.
Que Carlos HABLE en voz baja. | May (Have) Carlos speak in a whisper.
Que ella HABLE en voz alta. | May she speak aloud. (Have her speak aloud.)
Que Uds. HABLEN en voz alta. | May you (all) speak aloud (in a high voice).
Que ellos HABLEN en voz alta. | May they speak aloud.

(ayudar) AYUDE Ud. | (to help) Help
Que Dios nos ayude en momentos difíciles. | May God help us in difficult moments.
Que los ricos ayuden a los pobres. | May the rich help the poor.
(beber) BEBA Ud. | (to drink) Drink
Que ellos beban este vino, que es mi sangre. | May they drink this wine, which is my blood.
(recibir) RECIBA Ud. | (to receive) Receive
Que Ud. reciba las cenizas. | May you receive the ashes.
Que ellos reciban el Espíritu Santo. | May they receive the Holy Spirit.
(llegar) LLEGUE Ud. | (to arrive) Arrive
Que los padres lleguen a las diez. | May the parents arrive at 10:00.
(ser) SEA Ud. | (to be) May you be
Que los padrinos SEAN puntuales. | May the godparents be punctual.
(venir) VENGA Ud. | (to come) Come
Que Uds. VENGAN a la iglesia a las diez en punto. | May you come to the church at 10:00 on the dot.
(decir) DIGA Ud. | (to say) Say (speak)
Que el niño diga la verdad. | May the child say the truth.
(bendecir) BENDIGA Ud. | (to bless) Bless
Que Cristo los bendiga. | May Christ bless them.
(hacer) HAGA Ud. | (to do or make) Do
Que ellos hagan todo para Ud. | May they do everything for you.
(guardar) GUARDE Ud. | (to guard, keep) Watch
Que el pastor guarde sus ovejas. | May the shepherd watch his sheep.

(Que el Señor) " te bendiga y te guarde,
...(que) haga resplendor su rostro sobre ti,
y te conceda lo que pidas, vuelva hacia
ti su rostro y te dé la paz."

"May the Lord bless you and keep you,
may the Lord make his face to shine upon you,
may He give you what you wish and turn
His face toward you and give you peace."
(Numbers, 7: 25-26)

THE SUBJUNCTIVE WITH WISHING AND HOPING

Quiero ayudar.
Quiero QUE UD....
Quiero QUE UD. AYUDE.
Ellos quieren comer.
Ellos quieren que Ud. COMA.
El cura quiere regresar.
El cura quiere que Ud. REGRESE.
El cura quiere que Ana REGRESE
El cura quiere que yo REGRESE a Cristo.
El cura quiere que ellos REGRESEN a Cristo.
El cura quiere que nosotros REGRESEMOS a Cristo.

I want to help.
I want you...
I want YOU to help.
They want to eat.
They want you to eat.
The priest wants to return.
The priest wants you to return.
The priest want Ana to return.
The priest wants me to return to Christ.
The priest wants them to return to Christ.
The priest wants us to return to Christ.

Queremos que Ud. TENGA la licencia.
Queremos que ellas TENGAN el coche.
Queremos que Mario DIGA las palabras.
Anita quiere que yo EXPLIQUE el dogma.
Mi hermanito quiere que yo le DÉ un regalo.
Los estudiantes quieren que Ud. LEA la lección.
Nuestro profesor quiere que nosotros ESCRIBAMOS.
Quiero que Ud. TOME (BEBA) un café conmigo.
La profesora cruel quiere que ESCUCHEMOS las cintas.
Esperar
(yo) Espero el tren. Ella espera el taxi.
Ud. espera a la profesora. Espero a mi tía. (3-F)
Espero salir a las tres.
Ellos esperan ayudar a los pobres.
Espero QUE ELLOS AYUDEN a los pobres.
Ellos esperan QUE YO SALGA a las tres.
La madrina espera que todo ESTÉ en orden.
El doctor espera que su paciente ESTÉ mejor.
Espero que los padres PIENSEN en la importancia del bautismo.

We want you to have the license.
We want them to have the car.
We want Mario to say the words.
Anita wants me to explain dogma.
My little brothers wants me to give him a gift.
The students want you to read the lesson.
Our teacher wants us to write.
I want you to drink some coffee with me.
The cruel professor wants us to listen to the tapes.
to hope or to wait for
I wait for the train. She waits for the taxi.
You wait for the professor. I wait for my aunt.
I hope to leave at 3:00.
They hope to help the poor.
I hope that they help the poor.
They hope that I leave at 3:00.
The godmother hopes that everything is in order.
The doctor hopes that his patient his better.
I hope the parents think about the importance of baptism.

Esperamos que Ud. TENGA el dinero.
El señor García espera que el mecánico HAGA un buen trabajo.
Ud. espera que nosotros DEJEMOS la vieja vida.

We hope that you have the money.
Mr. Garcia hopes that the mechanic does a good job.
You hope that we leave the old life.

THE SUBJUNCTIVE WITH EXPRESSIONS OF EMOTION AND DOUBT

Me alegro de que....
Siento que...
Me gusta que...
Dudo que...
Me alegro de que los señores García LLEGUEN a tiempo.
Siento que su abuelo ESTÉ enfermo.
Dudo que Luisa VENGA a las diez.
Me gusta que el cura HABLE español.

I am happy that...
I am sorry that....
I like (the fact) that...
I doubt that...
I am happy that Mr. and Mrs. García arrive on time.
I am sorry that your grandfather is sick.
I doubt that Luisa will come at 10:00.
I like (the fact) that the priest speaks Spanish.

IMPERSONAL PHRASES WITH THE INFINITIVE OR THE SUBJUNCTIVE

Es necesario rezar todos los días.
Es preciso planear la ceremonia.
Es posible comenzar una nueva vida en Cristo.
Es imposible dormir con tanto ruido.
Es mejor usar el diccionario.
Es importante venir a la rectoría.
Es lástima llegar tarde.

It is necessary to pray every day.
It is necessary to plan the ceremony.
It is possible to start a new life in Christ.
It is impossible to sleep with so much noise.
It is better to use the dictionary.
It is important to come to the rectory.
It is a shame (pity) to arrive late.

Es importante que Ud. LEA la lección.
Es preciso que yo ESTÉ unos minutos con el enfermo.
Es imposible que la señora VAYA a la tienda ahora.
Es mejor que nosotros USEMOS el diccionario.
Es necesario que Ud. COMIENCE una nueva vida.
Es preciso que yo RECE todos los días.
Es posible que los niños VUELVAN tarde.
Es lástima que la novia LLEGUE tarde.

It is important for you to read the lesson.
It is necessary that I be a few minutes with the sick man.
It is impossible for the woman to go to the store now.
It is better that we use a dictionary.
It is necessary for you to start a good life.
It is important that I pray every day.
It is possible that the children will return late.
It is a shame that the bride arrives late.

(Complete the following pattern drill using the subjunctive. The correct answer will follow)

(repetir) Quiero que Ud.......
(Quiero que Ud. repita.)
(comer) Quiero que Carlos....

(to repeat) I want you ...
(I want you to repeat.)
(to eat) I want Carlos ...

(Quiero que Carlos coma.)	*(I want Carlos to eat.)*
(beber) Espero que Ud....	(to drink) I hope that you...
(Espero que Ud. beba.)	*(I hope that you drink)*
(comprar) Es mejor que ellos...	(to buy) It is better that they...
(Es mejor que ellos compren.)	*(It is better that they buy.)*
(venir) Siento que mi tío no...	(to come) I'm sorry that my uncle...
(Siento que mi tío no venga.)	*(I'm sorry that my uncle isn't coming.)*
(dar un regalo) Ellos esperan que yo les.......	(to give a gift) They hope that I will give them...
(Ellos esperan que yo les dé un regalo.)	*(They hope that I will give them a gift.)*
(escuchar las cintas) Es necesario que nosotros...	(to listen to the tapes) It is necessary that we...
(Es necesario que nosotros escuchemos las cintas.)	*(It is necessary that we listen to the tapes.)*
(pensar) Ella quiere que sus hijos...	(to think) She wants her children to...
(Ella quiere que sus hijos piensen.)	*(She wants her children to think.)*
(no trabajar) Es lástima que mis amigos...	(to work) It is a shame that my friends...
(Es lástima que mis amigos no trabajen.)	*(It is a shame that my friends do not work.)*
(llegar tarde) Es lástima que el avión...	(to arrive late) It is a shame that the plane...
(Es lástima que el avión llegue tarde.)	*(It is a shame that the plane arrives late.)*

DIÁLOGO: EL SANTO O EL CUMPLEAÑOS

Luis habla con una amiga de trabajo, Ana
que nació en Nueva York de padres puertorriqueños.
Están en un supermercado.

ANA--¡Hola, Luis!   Veo que Ud. compra una torta (tarta,
un pastel). ¿ Va Ud. a comprar velitas también?

LUIS-- No, no compro velitas porque no es
mi cumpleaños.   Mi cumpleaños es el cinco de enero.
Hoy es el día de mi santo (6-c) y tenemos una fiesta en casa
a las ocho. Quiero que Ud. venga y conozca a mi familia.

ANA--Me gustaría ir. En mi familia ya no celebramos esa
tradición. Solamente tenemos fiestas para los cumpleaños,
que es la costumbre de los Estados Unidos.

LUIS--Me alegro que Ud. pueda venir. Me gusta que
mi familia todavía conserve tradiciones mexicanas.
Espero que a Ud. le guste la fiesta. Hasta pronto.

DIALOG: SAINT'S DAY OR BIRTHDAY

Luis speaks with a friend from work, Ana,
who was born in New York of Puerto Rican parents,
They are in a supermarket.

Hello, Luis! I see you are buying a cake.
Are you going to buy candles too?

No, I'm not buying candles because it isn't
my birthday. My birthday is January 5.
Today is my saint's day and we are having a party at home
at 8:00. I want you to come and meet my family.

I would like to go. In my family we no longer celebrate that
tradition. We only have parties for birthdays,
which is the custom in the United States.

I am happy you can come. I like (the fact) that
my family keeps Mexican traditions.
I hope you like the party. Until later.

¿PUEDE UD. COMPRENDER? LOS HISPANOS EN LOS ESTADOS UNIDOS

(Repita Ud. el vocabulario nuevo)

el desfile
los países hispanoamericanos
las carrozas
los trajes típicos
las banderas nacionales
tocar música
el origen
refugiados
exiliados
inmigrantes
ciudadanos
aculturación
los americanos (los norteamericanos)
americanizado

(Escuche Ud. con ciudado y conteste Ud. CIERTO o FALSO después a las preguntas)

Hay gran diversidad entre los hispanos que viven en los Estados Unidos. En muchas ciudades americanas celebran el Día de la Raza (el 12 de octubre) con desfiles. Todos los países hispanoamericanos y ex-colonias, como por ejemplo, las Islas Filipinas, tienen carrozas en los desfiles con personas en trajes típicos y banderas nacionales. Muchos bailan y tocan música tradicional.

Muchos hispanos son refugiados políticos de la América Central, exiliados de Cuba o inmigrantes de otros países que vienen buscando oportunidades y trabajo.
Desde 1917 los puertorriqueños son ciudadanos americanos y no tienen problemas con la "migra", la inmigración. Los méxico-americanos (chicanos), personas de Texas, Arizona, Nuevo México y California, cuyos padres nacieron en territorio americano, también son ciudadanos.

CAN YOU UNDERSTAND? HISPANICS IN THE UNITED STATES

(Repeat the new vocabulary)

the parade
Latinamerican countries
the parade floats
traditional suits (costumes)
the national flags
to play music
origin
refugees
exiles
immigrants
citizens
acculturation
Americans
Americanized

(Listen carefully and answer TRUE or FALSE after the questions)

There is a great diversity among Hispanics that live in the United States. In many American cities they celebrate Día de la Raza (October 12) with parades. All Latin American countries and former colonies, for example, the Philippines, have floats in the parades with people in typical costumes and national flags. Many dance and play traditional music.

Many Hispanics are political refugees from Central American, exiles from Cuba or immigrants from other countries that come looking for opportunities and work. Since 1917 Puerto Ricans are American citizens and they don't have immigration problems. Mexican-Americans (Chicanos), from Texas, Arizona, New Mexico and California, whose parents and grandparents were born in American territory, also are citizens.

La mayoría de los hispanos que viven en los Estados Unidos son de origen mexicano. Los méxicano-americanos tienen diferentes grados de aculteración: muchos hablan español y conservan las tradiciones pero otros son completemente americanizados y ya no hablan la lengua de sus abuelos.

The majority of Hispanics that live in the United States are of Mexican origin. Mexican-Americans have different grades of acculturation: some speak Spanish and conserve traditions but some are completely Americanized and no longer speak the language of their grandparents.

¿CIERTO O FALSO?

1. Los puertorriqueõs son ciudadanos americanos.
(CIERTO)

2. El Día de la Raza es el 16 de septiembre.
(FALSO--El Día de la Raza es el 12 de octubre.)

3. Usan carrozas en muchos desfiles.
(CIERTO)

4. La mayoría de los hispanos en este país son cubanos.
(FALSO--La mayoría es de origen mexicano.)

5. Entre los hispanos en los Estados Unidos hay diferentes grados de aculturación.
(CIERTO)

TRUE OR FALSE?

1. Puerto Ricans are American citizens.
(True)

2. Dia de la Raza is September 16.
(False--It is October 12.)

3. They use floats in many parades.
(True)

4. The majority of Hispanics in this country are Cubans.
(False--The majority is of Mexican origin.)

5. Among Hispanics in the United States there are different grades of acculturation.
(True)

GRAMMAR

6-A   FAVOR DE + infinitive = *Do me the favor of... (please...)*

This is the shortened form of *Hágame el favor de...* (Do me the favor of...). It is an easy way for beginning Spanish speakers to give a command by using *favor de* with almost any infinitive. However, because it involves more syllables than the command, it is less used by native speakers although it is seen sometimes on signs. Some examples are:

> Favor de escribir la carta.   (Do me the favor of writing the letter.)
> Favor de decirme la verdad. (Do me the favor of telling me the truth.)

6-B THE SUBJUNCTIVE MOOD

In Spanish the speaker uses the INDICATIVE mood, (all the verbs taught so far), to express what is considered a fact.

Cuando José era pequeño vivía en México. (When Jose was small, he used to live in Mexico.)
Ellos son mecánicos y buscan trabajo. (They are mechanics and are looking for work.)
Vamos a comer a las dos y media. (We are going to eat at 2:30.)

The SUBJUNCTIVE mood is used when there is a possibility that the action may not take place. Part of the difficulty of this concept to English speakers is the fact that while the subjunctive is widely used in Spanish, it is rarely used in English, and almost never used correctly. *John goes to the store* or *I believe that John goes to the store* is seen as a fact and takes the INDICATIVE. However, *I want John to go to the store* or *I doubt that John goes to the store* is seen as SUBJUNCTIVE because there is no certainty that John wants to go anywhere. There are several categories that usually take the subjunctive. In this chapter the most important ones, direct commands, indirect commands, wishing, hoping, emotion, doubt and impersonal phrases will be covered. Learning the SUBJUNCTIVE takes much practice.

Except for the commands, all SUBJUNCTIVE verbs are in 1) a dependent clause following certain phrases with 2)QUE + a change of subject.

Quiero comer. (I want to eat.) INDICATIVE because it doesn't satisfy #1 and #2.

Alberto quiere QUE YO COMA. (Alberto wants me to eat/ wishes that I eat.) SUBJUNCTIVE because *que* introduces the dependent clause and *yo* is a new subject. NOTE that in English an infinitive may sometimes be used where in Spanish the SUBJUNCTIVE BE USED.

COMMANDS WITH USTED AND USTEDES

Take the present tense verb form of *yo*, drop the *O* and add *E* for -AR verbs and *A* for -ER and -IR verbs.

HABLAR-to speak	hablo---habl----HABLE	DECIR-to say	digo---dig-----DIGA
COMER-to eat	como---com----COMA	HACER-to do	hago---hag----HAGA
VIVIR-to eat	vivo-----viv-----VIVA	PENSAR-to think	pienso-piens--PIENSE

To make the command in English one drops the pronoun: You eat---Eat.
In Spanish one uses the subjunctive form before the pronoun: Ud. habla---HABLE Ud. (Speak)
Ud. no come---No COMA Ud. (Don't eat)

The Uds. command is the same as Ud. but add *N*: Viva Ud. ----VIVAN Uds. (Live)
No hable Ud.--No HABLEN Uds. (Don't speak)

CONJUGATING THE PRESENT SUBJUNCTIVE

	HABLAR-to speak	COMER-to eat	VIVIR-to live	DECIR-to say	PENSAR-to think	VOLVER-to return
yo	hable	coma	viva	diga	piense	vuelva
tú	hables	comas	vivas	digas	pienses	vuelvas
Ud.	hable	coma	viva	diga	piense	vuelva
nosotros	hablemos	comamos	vivamos	digamos	pensemos	volvamos
Uds.	hablen	coman	vivan	digan	piensen	vuelvan

SOME IRREGULAR VERBS

HACER-to do	haga, hagas, haga, hagamos, hagan
PONER-to put	ponga, pongas, ponga, pongamos, pongan
TENER-to have	tenga, tengas, tenga, tengamos, tengan
SALIR-to leave	salga, salgas, salga, salgamos salgan
VENIR-to come	venga, vengas, venga, vengamos, vengan
CONOCER-to know	conozca, conozcas, conozca, conozcamos, conozcan
QUERER-to want	quiera, quieras, quiera, queramos, quieran
PODER-to be able	pueda, puedas, pueda, podamos, puedan
PREFERIR-to prefer	prefiera, prefieras, prefiera, prefiramos, prefieran
DORMIR-to sleep	duerma, duermas, duerma, durmamos, duerman
PEDIR-to ask for	pida, pidas, pida, pidamos, pidan
DAR- to give	dé, des, dé, demos, den
IR-to go	vaya, vayas, vaya, vayamos, vayan
SER-to be	sea, seas, sea, seamos, sean
ESTAR-to be	esté, estés, esté, estemos, estén
SABER-to know	sepa, sepas, sepa, sepamos, sepan

NOTE that as with the imperfect tense, the *yo* and *Ud.* forms of the SUBJUNCTIVE are the same. Again, this makes *You-I* conversation a bit easier. Only *DAR* and *ESTAR* carry written accents.

SPELLING CHANGES :	EXPLICAR-to explain	explique, expliques, expique, expliquemos, expliquen
	BUSCAR-to look for	busque....
	TOCAR-to play music	toque...
	LLEGAR-to arrive	llegue, llegues, llegue, lleguemos, lleguen
	PAGAR-to pay	pague...

INDIRECT COMMANDS: QUE + subjunctive

Que la señora **venga** temprano. (Have the lady come early/ may the lady come early.)
Que los niños **toquen** el piano. (Have the children play the piano/ May the children play the piano.)

SUBJUNCTIVE WITH WISHING AND HOPING

Some common verbs that will take subjunctive:
QUERER- to want
DESEAR-to desire
ESPERAR-to hope
PREFERIR-to prefer

Quiero que Ud. **diga** la verdad. (I want you to say the truth.)
Ellos desean que él **haga** el trabajo. (They want him to do the work.)
Esperamos que Uds. **vengan** pronto. (We hope that you come soon.)
Prefiero que Carmen **lea** el libro. (I prefer that Carmen read the book.)

SUBJUNCTIVE WITH EMOTION AND DOUBT

ALEGRARSE DE-to be happy
SENTIR-to be sorry
GUSTARLE-to like
DUDAR-to doubt

Me alegro de que Ud. **sepa** la respuesta. (I am happy that you know the answer.)
Siento que ellos **salgan** ahora.   (I am sorry that they are leaving now.)
Me gusta que el avión **llegue**. (I'm glad, I like that the plane is arriving.)
Dudo que ellos **escuchen** las cintas cada día. (I doubt that they listen to the tapes each day.)

IMPERSONAL PHRASES

The INFINITIVE is used with these phrases UNLESS A SUBJECT IS INTRODUCED.

Es necesario comer. (It is necesary to eat)   BUT   Es necesario que Ud. **coma**. (It is necessary for you to eat.)

Some impersonal phrases that take subjunctive:

Es necesario que...	(it is necessary)	Es necesario que ellos **practiquen** inglés. (It is necessary for them to practice English.)
Es preciso que...	(it is necessary)	Es preciso que yo **escriba** a máquina. (It is necessary for me to type.)
Es posible que...	(it is possible)	Es posible que **vayamos** a Cuba. (It is possible for us to go to Cuba.)
Es imposible que...	(it is impossible)	Es imposible que él **viva** aquí. (It is impossible for him to live here.)
Es mejor que ...	(it is better)	Es mejor que ellos **hagan** *la*s preguntas. (It is better for them to ask questions.)
Es importante que...	(it is important)	Es importante que mi familia **esté** aquí. (It is important that my family be here.)
Es lástima que...	(it is a shame, pity)	Es lástima que ella **esté** enferma. (It is a shame that she is sick.)

Chapter 6 - ASH WEDNESDAY AND LENT

VOCABULARY AND CULTURAL NOTES

a) *pensar en* (to think about)   Pienso en mi familia. (I think about my family.)   The verb can also introduce the infinitive:

Pienso ir a la tienda. (I am thinking about going to the store.) Piensan volver a casa. (They think about returning home.)

b) *un buen cristiano* (a good Christian)   This is an example of the few apocopated adjectives that have a shortened form when used BEFORE a masculine singular noun. Other examples are: *malo---un mal hombre* (bad---a bad man), *primero--el primer piso* (first---the first floor), *tercero--el tercer libro* (third--the third book). If these adjectives are used after the noun, there is no change (un cristiano bueno) or if used before or after a feminine word or a masculine plural (*una buena cristiana, una cristiana buena, unos buenos cristianos, unos cristianos buenos*).

c) *el día de santo* (the saint's day). In most Spanish-speaking countries people are given names of Catholic saints.   If children are not named for a family member or friend, they may be given the name of the saint of the day they were born. In some countries the saint's day is more important than the birthday. There may be family gatherings for either or both occasions, but except for children or the rich, most don't expect gifts for both days. *El cumpleaños* (literally, *completes years)*, is an example of a compound word, almost all of which are masculine and end with the letter *s*. Others are: *el paraguas* (umbrella), *el abrelatas* (can-opener). The plural of such words is indicated only by the article: *los cumpleaños* (the birthdays).

CHAPTER 7

PALM SUNDAY

TAPESCRIPT

REVIEW OF INFINITIVE STRUCTURES AND PRESENT TENSE

(Listen and Repeat)

Voy a necesitar algo.
(yo) necesito   Ud. necesita
Quiero regresar a casa.
(yo) regreso   Ud. regresa
No necesito comer nada.
No como nada   Ud. no come nada
Me gusta ayudar a la gente.
(yo) ayudo   Ud. ayuda
Sé manejar un carro.
(yo) manejo   Ud. maneja
Puedo escribir la carta.
(yo) escribo   Ud. escribe
Prefiero tomar un café.
(yo) tomo   Ud. toma
Tengo que recibir el correo.
(yo) recibo   Ud. recibe
Pienso ir de vacaciones. (7-a)
(yo) voy   Ud. va

I am going to need something.
I need   You need
I want to return home.
I return   You return
I don't need to eat anything.
I don't eat anything.   You don't eat anything.
I like to help people.
I help   You help
I know how to drive a car.
I drive   You drive
I can (am able to) write the letter.
I write   You write
I prefer to drink some coffee.
I drink   You drink
I must receive the mail.
I receive   You receive
I am thinking of going on vacation.
I go   You go

(Substitute the "yo" form for the given verbs. The correct answer will follow.)

Elena bebe---yo	Elena drinks--I
(yo bebo)	*I drink*
La enfermera ayuda---yo	The nurse helps---I
(yo ayudo)	*I help*
Mi abuelo va--yo	My grandfather goes---I
(yo voy)	*I go*
El mecánico escribe---yo	The mechanic writes---I
(yo escribo)	*I write*
La enfermera piensa---yo	The nurse thinks---I
(yo pienso)	*I think*

(Listen and repeat)

(ser) Soy católico.	(to be) I am a Catholic.
Carlos es católico.	Carlos is Catholic.
(estar) Estoy enferma.	(to be) I am sick.
Mi tío está enfermo.	My uncle is sick.
(salir) Salgo de la tienda.	(to leave) I leave the store.
Mi hijo sale de la tienda.	My son leaves the store.
(volver) Vuelvo a México.	(to return) I return to Mexico.
El profesor vuelve a México.	The professor returns to Mexico.

PRESENT TENSE REVIEW WITH DIRECT OBJECT PRONOUNS (7-A)

(tener) Tengo el libro.---LO tengo.	(to have) I have the book.---I have it.
Carlos tiene el libro.--Carlos LO tiene.	Carlos has the book.--Carlos has it.
(ver) Veo la película.---LA veo.	(to see) I see the movie.--I see it.
Carlos ve la película.--Carlos LA ve.	Carlos sees the movie.--Carlos sees it.
(hacer) Hago el trabajo.---LO hago.	(to make, do) I do the work.---I do it.
Carlos hace el trabajo.---Carlos LO hace.	Carlos does the work.--Carlos does it.
(poner) Pongo los libros aquí.---LOS pongo aquí.	(to put) I put the books here.---I put them here.
Carlos pone los libros aquí.--Carlos LOS pone aquí.	Carlos puts the books here.--Carlos puts them here.
(querer) Quiero las cartas.---LAS quiero.	(to want) I want the letters.---I want them.
Carlos quiere las cartas.--Carlos LAS quiere.	Carlos wants the letters.---Carlos wants them.
(decir) (yo) no digo la verdad.---(yo) no LA digo.	(to say, tell) I don't say the truth.--I don't say it.
Carlos no dice la verdad.---Carlos no LA dice.	Carlos doesn't say the truth.--Carlos doesn't say it.

(dar) No doy el dinero.---No LO doy.
      Carlos no da el dinero.---Carlos no LO da.

(to give) I don't give the money.--I don't give it.
      Carlos doesn't give the money.--Carlos doesn't give it.

(Substitute with the direct object pronoun. The correct answer will follow)

Veo la luz.-------(*La veo.*)
Compro los libros.---(*Los compro.*)
Como helado.------(*Lo como.*)
Miro los coches.---(*Los miro.*)
Digo unas palabras.---(*Las digo.*)
Hago el café.---(*Lo hago.*)
Veo la película.---(*La veo.*)
Digo las palabras.---(*Las digo.*)

I see the light.----(*I see it.*)
I buy the books.-----(*I buy them.*)
I eat ice cream.----(*I eat it.*)
I look at (watch) the cars.---(*I watch them.*)
I say some words.---(*I say them.*)
I make coffee.---(*I make it.*)
I see the film.---(*I see it.*)
I say the words.---(*I say them.*)

PEOPLE AS DIRECT OBJECT PRONOUNS

(Listen and repeat)

Conozco a Carlos.---LO conozco.
Conozco a Marta.---LA conozco.
Conozco a ellos.---LOS conozco.
Conozco a ellas.---LAS conozco.
Conozco a Ud. (hombre)---LO conozco.
Conozco a Uds. (hombres)---LOS conozco.
Conozco a Ud. (mujer)----LA conozco.
Conozco a Uds. (mujeres)---LAS conozco.
(Carlos conoce a mí).----Carlos ME conoce.
(Carlos conoce a ti.)----Carlos TE conoce.
(Carlos conoce a nosotros.)---Carlos NOS conoce.

I know Carlos.---I know him.
I know Marta.----I know her.
I know them.---I know them.
I know them.---I know them.
I know you (a man)---I know you.
I know you (pl. men)---I know you.
I know you (a woman)---I know you.
I know you (women only)---I know you.
Carlos knows me---Carlos knows me.
Carlos know you (familiar)---Carlos knows you.
Carlos knows us---Carlos knows us.

(Substitute with the direct object pronouns. The correct answer will follow.)

Ana ve a mí.----(*Ana me ve.*)
El rey mira a los muchachos.---(*El rey los mira.*)
Vemos al rey.----(*Lo vemos.*)
No conocemos a la señora.---(*No la conocemos.*)
Ellos quieren a sus hijas.---(*Ellos las quieren.*)
Ellos quieren a mí.---(*Ellos me quieren.*)
Ellos quieren a Ud. (hombre)---(*Ellos lo quieren.*)

Ana sees me.----(*Ana sees me.*)
The king looks at the boys.---(*The king looks at them.*)
We see the king.---(*We see him.*)
We do not know the woman.---(*We do not know her.*)
They love their daughters.---(*They love them.*)
They love me.---(*They love me.*)
They love you (a man).---(*They love you.*)

Ellos quieren a nosotros.---(*Ellos nos quieren.*)   They love us.---(*They love us.*)

PRESENT AND PRETERITE TENSES COMPARED   (7-B)

(Listen and repeat)

(tomar) Hoy (yo) tomo---AYER TOMÉ
(usar)   Hoy uso---Ayer usé
(trabajar) Hoy trabajo---Ayer trabajé
(ayudar) Hoy ayudo---Ayer ayudé
(dejar) Hoy dejo----Ayer dejé
(regresar) Hoy regreso---Ayer regresé
(comenzar) Hoy comienzo---Ayer comencé
(comer) Hoy como---AYER COMÍ
(beber) Hoy bebo---Ayer bebí
(aprender) Hoy aprendo---Ayer aprendí
(creer) Hoy creo---Ayer creí
(conocer) Hoy conozco---Ayer conocí
(recibir) Hoy recibo---AYER RECIBÍ
(vivir) Hoy vivo---Ayer viví

(to take, eat,drink) Today I take--Yesterday I took
(to use) Today I use---Yesterday I used
(to work) Today I work---Yesterday I worked
(to help) Today I help--Yesterday I worked
(to leave) Today I leave---Yesterday I left
(to return) Today I return---Yesterday I returned
(to begin) Today I begin--Yesterday I began
(to eat) Today I eat---Yesterday I ate
(to drink) Today I drink---Yesterday I drank
(to learn) Today I learn---Yesterday I learned
(to believe) Today I believe---Yesterday I believed
(to know) Today I know---Yesterday I met
(to receive) Today I receive---Yesterday I received
(to live) Today I live--Yesterday I lived

(tomar) Hoy Ud. toma---ANOCHE Ud. TOMÓ
(entrar) Hoy Ud. entra---Anoche Ud. entró
(comer) Hoy Ud. come---Anoche Ud. COMIÓ
(aprender) Hoy Ud. aprende---Anoche Ud. aprendió
(recibir) Hoy Ud. recibe---Anoche Ud. RECIBIÓ
(vivir) Hoy Ud. vive---Anoche vivió

(to take) Today you take---Last night you took
(to enter) Today you enter---Last night you entered
(to eat) Today you eat---Last night you ate
(to learn) Today you learn---Last night you learned
(to receive) Today you receive---Last night you received
(to live) Today you live---Last night you lived

(Answer the questions affirmatively. The correct answer will follow.)

¿Ayudó Ud.? (*Sí, yo ayudé*)
¿Comió ella? (*Sí, ella comió*)
¿Trabajó él.? (*Sí, él trabajó*)
¿Bebió Ud.? (*Sí, bebí*)
¿Nació Ud? (*Sí, nací*)

Did you help? (*Yes, I helped*)
Did she eat?   (*Yes, she ate*)
Did he work? (*Yes, he worked*)
Did you drink? (*Yes, I drank*)
Were you born? (*Yes, I was born*)

PHRASES ASSOCIATED WITH THE PRETERITE   (Repetition)

ayer	yesterday
anoche	last night
ayer a las tres y media	yesterday at 3:30
el año pasado	last year
la semana pasada	last week
hace una semana	a week ago
hace dos años	two years ago

MORE VERBS IN THE PRETERITE (7-C)   (Repetition)

(estar) estoy----estuve	(to be) I am---I was
está-----estuvo	you are---You were
(tener) tengo---tuve	(to have) I have---I had
tiene---tuvo	you have---You had
(venir) vengo---vine	(to come) I come---I came
viene---vino	you come---you came
(hacer) hago---hice	(to make, do) I do---I did
hace----hizo	you do------You did
(poner) pongo--puse	(to put) I put---I put
pone----puso	you put---you put
(decir) digo---dije	(to say) I say----I said
dice----dijo	you say----You said
(ser) soy ---fui es----fue	(to be) I am---I was you are----you were
(ir) voy---fui va----fue	(to go) I go---I went you go----you went
(dar) doy---di	(to give) I give---I gave
da---dio	you give---you gave
(ver) veo---vi	(to see) I see---I saw
ve---vio	you see---you saw

(Listen and repeat the sentences.)

Jesús entró en Jerusalém y saludó a la gente.	Jesus entered Jerusalem and greeted the people.
El ladrón robó el dinero de la gente.	The thief robbed the money of the people.
Jesús envió a dos discípulos.	Jesus sent two disciples.
La señora compró regalos para sus nietos.	The woman bought gifts for her grandchildren.
Jesús curó a los enfermos y ayudó a los pobres.	Jesus cured the ill and helped the poor.
El santo hizo varios milagros.	The saint made several miracles.

Mi amigo me dio el dinero.	My friend gave me the money.
Cristo sufrió con las manos clavadas en la cruz.	Christ suffered with his hands nailed to the cross.
Alicia vino y puso sus cosas en la silla.	Alice came and put her things on the chair.
Cristo recibió insultos y una corona de espinas.	Christ received insults and a crown of thorns.
El Salvador predicó un mensaje de paz.	The Savior preached a message of peace.

DIRECT OBJECT SUBSTITUTION WITH PRETERITE VERBS

La santa hizo un milagro.---(*La santa lo hizo.*)	The saint made a miracle.--(*The saint made it.*)
La santa hizo varios milagros.---(*La santa los hizo.*)	The saint made several miracles.--(*The saint made them.*)
Alicia puso sus cosas aquí.---(*Alicia las puso aquí.*)	Alice put her things here.--(*Alice put them here.*)
El ladrón robó el dinero.---(*El ladrón lo robó.*)	The thief robbed the money.--(*The thief robbed it.*)
Cristo no tuvo trono.---(*Cristo no lo tuvo.*)	Christ did not have a throne.---(*Christ did not have it.*)
Jesús recibió una corona de espinas.--(*Jesús la recibió.*)	Jesus received a crown of thorns.--(*Jesus received it.*)

ADVERBS WITH --mente (7-D)

(Listen and repeat)

rápida	fast, rapid
rápidamente	rapidly
lenta	slow
lentamente	slowly
normal	normal
normalmente	normally

(Make the adverb from the feminine form of the adjective. The correct answer will follow)

general-----(*generalmente*)	general---(*generally*)
simple-----(*simplemente*)	simple---(*simply*)
frecuente---(*frecuentemente*)	frequent---(*frequently*)
clara----(*claramente*)	clear---(*clearly*)
fácil----(*fácilmente*)	easy----(*easily*)
constante---(*constantemente*)	constant--(*constantly*)

DIÁLOGO: UN VIAJE A COLOMBIA

(Escuche y repita el nuevo vocabulario)

¡Qué lugar!
¡Qué mujer!
¡Qué lindo!
 Fíjese! (imagínese!)
la prueba
la fe y la devoción
los mineros
la vista
una montaña de sal
la cultura indígena
la cultura de los indios
 ¿Dónde está Zipaquirá?
--Está cerca de Bogotá.
--No está lejos de Bogotá.
--Está a cuarenta minutos de Bogotá.
--Está a treinta millas de Bogotá.

DIÁLOGO (Dos personas hablan)

LUIS-- Dónde estuvo Ud. el mes pasado?
No la vi.

SONIA--Pasé mis vacaciones visitando a mis parientes
en Colombia.

LUIS-¡Qué suerte!   ¿Qué vio y qué hizo?

SONIA--Visité el Museo del Oro de Bogotá.   Qué lugar!
Tiene arte de muchas diferentes culturas indígenas.

LUIS-- ¿Le gustó Bogotá?

SONIA--Sí, me gustó mucho. Es una capital moderna
y antigua (vieja). Subimos a la Montaña de Montserrate
para ver la ciudad. ¡Qué vista!

DIALOG: A TRIP TO COLOMBIA

(Listen and repeat the new vocabulary)

What a place!
What a woman!
How pretty!
Just imagine!
the sample, proof
faith and devotion
the mineros
the view
a mountain of salt
the indigenous culture
the culture of the Indians
Where is Zipaquirá?
--It is near Bogota.
--It isn't far from Bogota.
--It is 40 minutes from Bogota.
--It is 30 miles from Bogota.

DIALOG   (Two people talk)

Where were you last month?
I didn't see you.

I spent my vacation visiting my relatives
in Colombia.

How lucky! What did you see and do?

I visited the Museum of Gold in Bogota. What a place!
It has art of many different Indian cultures.

Did you like Bogota?

Yes, I liked it very much. It is a modern yet old
capital. We went up to Monserrate Mountain
in order to see the city. What view!

LUIS-- ¿Qué más hizo?

What else did you do?

SONIA--Visité la Catedral de Zipaquirá que está a cuarenta minutos de la capital. Fíjese: la catedral fue tallada por los mineros en una montaña de sal. ¡Qué prueba de fe y devoción!

I visited the Cathedral of Zipaquirá that is 40 minutes from the capital. Just imagine: the Cathedral carved by the miners in a mountain of salt. What a proof of faith and devotion!

DIRECT OBJECT PRONOUNS WITH INFINITIVES

(Listen and repeat)

LO hago.   LO hice.
Quiero hacerLO. LO quiero hacer.
Ana quiere comprarLA. Ana LA quiere comprar.
Vamos a usarlos.   Los vamos a usar.
La hermana puede vernos.   La hermana nos puede ver.
Ud. sabe manejarlo. Ud. lo sabe manejar.
Debo leerlas. Las debo leer.

I do it. I did it.
I want to do it. (2 ways)
Ana wants to buy it. (2 ways)
We are going to use them.
The sister can see us.
You know how to drive it.
I ought to read them.

¿PUEDE UD. COMPRENDER? LOS GALÁPAGOS

CAN YOU UNDERSTAND? GALAPAGOS

(Repita Ud. el vocabulario)

(Repeat the vocabulary)

el fraile dominico (7-b)
navegar---navegando
llevar--llevaron
descubrir--descubrió
¿Dónde están los Galápagos?
--Están al sur de México.
--Están al norte del Perú.
--Están al oeste del Ecuador.
--No están al este.
de origen volcánico
las tortugas enormes (grandes)
el nombre actual
extraño (raro)
los (las) turistas
los (las) naturalistas

the Dominican friar
to sail--sailing
to carry--carried
to discover--discovered
Where are the Galapagos?
--They are south of Mexico.
--They are north of Peru.
--They are west of Ecuador.
--They are not to the east.
of volcanic origin
large turtles
the present name
strange
tourists
naturalists

En el año 1535 Fray Tomás de Berlanga, un fraile dominico de España, salió de Panamá navegando hacia el sur, pero las corrientes llevaron su barco a una isla al oeste del Ecuador. Descubrió accidentalmente quince islas de origen volcánico con animales raros. El nombre actual, Galápagos, se refiere a las tortugas enormes que viven allá.

Charles Darwin visitó las islas que lo influyeron en su teoría del origen de los especies. Muchos turistas y naturalistas visitan las islas para estudiar las extrañas formas de vida.

(Conteste Ud. CIERTO o FALSO)

1) El hombre que descubrió los Galápagos fue un fraile franciscano. (FALSO--Fue un fraile dominico.)

2) Los Galápagos están al norte de Panamá.
(FALSO--Están al oeste del Ecuador.)

3) Charles Darwin aprendió mucho en Galápagos.
(CIERTO)

4) El nombre "Galápagos" se refiere a las tortugas enormes que viven allá.   (CIERTO)

5) Los turistas visitan las islas porque hay hoteles y playas bonitas.
(FALSO--Los turistas visitan las islas para estudiar las extrañas formas de vida.)

In the year 1535 Tomas de Berlanga, a Dominican friar from Spain, sailed from Panama towards the south, but currents carried his boat to an island west of Ecuador. He accidently discovered 15 islands of volcanic origin with strange animals. The present name, Galapagos, refers to the enormous turtles that live there.

Charles Darwin visited the islands that influenced him in his theory of the origin of species. Many tourists and naturalists come to the islands to study the strange forms of life.

(Answer TRUE or FALSE)

The man who discovered the Galapagos was a Franciscan friar. (FALSE--He was a Dominican friar.)

The Galapagos are north of Panama.
(FALSE--They are west of Ecuador.)

Charles Darwin learned a great deal in the Galapagos.
(TRUE)

The name "Galapagos" refers to the huge turtles that live there.   (TRUE)

Tourists visit the islands because there are beautiful hotels and beaches.
(FALSE--Tourists visit the islands to study the rare life forms.)

GRAMMAR

7-A DIRECT OBJECT PRONOUNS

The direct object pronouns in Spanish are LO and LOS (masculine) and LA and LAS (feminine). In Latin America they can refer to either people or things and PRECEDE THE CONJUGATED FORM OF THE VERB.

Juan lee el libro. (Juan reads the book.)------Juan **lo** lee. (Juan reads it.)
Juan lee los libros. (Juan reads the books.)---Juan **los** lee. (Juan reads them.)
Ellos no tienen la flor. (They don't have the flower.)--Ellos no **la** tienen. (They don't have it.)
Ellos no tienen las flores. (They don't have the flowers.)--Ellos no **las** tienen. (They don't have them.)
Vemos a Carmen. (We see Carmen.)------**La** vemos. (We see her.)
Vemos a las niñas. (We see the girls.)----**Las** vemos. (We see them.)
Vemos a Ud. (We see you.)-----**Lo** // **La** vemos. (We see you--masculine//feminine)
Ud. ve a Roberto. (You see Roberto.)---Ud. **lo** ve. (You see him.)
Ud. ve a los niños. (You see the children.)---Ud. **los** ve. (You see them.)

The pronouns ME, TE, NOS are the same forms for either direct or indirect objects. (See Chapter 4)
The following examples are all **direct object pronouns.**

Fernando **me** ve. (Fernando sees me.)
El señor **te** mira. (The man is looking at you.)
Ellos **nos** buscaron. (They looked for us.)
Mis abuelos **me** querían mucho. (My grandparents loved me very much.)

NOTE that the **a** before persons here is the **personal a** that does not translate into English. The **a** associated with the indirect object does **translate as** *to*. (See Chapter 3)

DIRECT OBJECT PRONOUN: In Spain LE / LES are the forms for the direct object *him* or masculine *you* or *they*. In Spain: Veo a mi padre. Le ve   (I see my father. I see him.)
In Latin America: Veo a mi padre. Lo veo. (I see my father. I see him.)

It is not a question of *right* or *wrong*. It is simply a regional preference. This grammar program uses the more common form from Latin America in the exercises.

7-B THE PRETERITE TENSE

The PRETERITE is the past tense used to express an action COMPLETED AT A DEFINITE TIME IN THE PAST.

	PRESENT		**PRETERITE**
(yo)	CANTO	(yo)	CANTÉ

(yo) CANTO
- I sing
- I do sing
- I am singing

(yo) CANTÉ
- I sang
- I did sing

Ud. CANTA
- You sing
- You do sing
- You are singing

Ud. CANTÓ
- You sang
- You did sing

REMINDER: *do* and *did* are most common in questions.
¿Cantó Ud.?　(Did you sing?)
--Sí, canté.　(Yes, I sang.)

NOTE: GUSTARLE-to like
Me gustó el libro.　(I liked the book.)
A él le gustó el libro.　(He liked the book.)
Me gustaron los libros. (I liked the books.)

PRETERITE OF REGULAR VERBS

	HABLAR	COMER	VIVIR	
yo	HABLÉ	COMÍ	VIVÍ	(I spoke, ate, lived)
tú	hablaste	comiste	viviste	(You [fam.] spoke, ate, lived)
Ud.	HABLÓ	COMIÓ	VIVIÓ	(You spoke, ate, lived)
nosotros	hablamos	comimos	vivimos	(We spoke, ate, lived)
Uds.	hablaron	comieron	vivieron	(You [pl.] spoke, ate, lived)

The PRETERITE has many irregular verbs and spelling changes. This chapter stresses the first and third person singular, (*yo, Ud. él, ella*), which is the reason for the capitalization in the above list. Both forms have a written accent on the final letter (Ó, É, Í). The correct pronunciation is especially important with regular -AR verbs to distinguish the person and the tense:

Yo HABLO. (I speak--present tense)　Ana HABLÓ. (Ana spoke--preterite tense)
Yo HABLÉ. (I spoke--preterite)　HABLE Ud. (Command: speak) [See Chapter 6]

The *nosotros* form for regular -AR and -IR verbs (-AMOS and -IMOS) is the same for the present and preterite but are generally understood by context. Chapter 8 of PASTORAL SPANISH continues the study of the PRETERITE tense and compares it with the imperfect tense. Chapter 10 also reviews the PRETERITE and drills the third person plural forms (*ellas, ellos, Uds.*).

ORTHOGRAPHIC (SPELLING) CHANGES

	EXPLICAR-to explain	LLEGAR-to arrive	COMENZAR-to begin	
yo	EXPLIQUÉ	LLEGUÉ	COMENCÉ	(I explained, arrived, began)
tú	explicaste	llegaste	comenzaste	(You [fam.] explained, arrived, began)
Ud.	explicó	llegó	comenzó	(You explained, arrived, began)
nosotros	explicamos	llegamos	comenzamos	(We explained, arrived, began)
Uds.	explicaron	llegaron	comenzaron	(You [pl.] explained, arrived, began)

7-C COMMON VERBS IRREGULAR IN THE PRETERITE

DAR- to give	DI, diste, DIO, dimos, dieron
HACER-to make , do	HICE, hiciste, HIZO, hicimos, hicieron
CREER-to believe	CREÍ, creiste, CREYÓ, creimos, creyeron
LEER-to read	LEÍ, leiste, LEYÓ, leimos, leyeron
TENER-to have	TUVE, tuviste, TUVO, tuvimos, tuvieron
ESTAR-to be	ESTUVE, estuviste, ESTUVO, estuvimos, estuvieron
PONER-to put	PUSE, pusiste, PUSO, pusimos, pusieron
VENIR-to come	VINE, viniste, VINO, vinimos, vinieron
PODER-to be able	PUDE, pudiste, PUDO, pudimos, pudieron
SABER-to know	SUPE, supiste, SUPO, supimos, supieron
QUERER-to want	QUISE, quisiste, QUISO, quisimos, quisieron
DECIR-to say	DI JE, dijiste, DIJO, dijimos, dijeron
IR-to go	FUI, fuiste, FUE, fuimos, fueron
SER-to be	FUI, fuiste, FUE, fuimos, fueron
DORMIR-to sleep	DORMÍ, dormiste, DURMIÓ, dormimos, durmieron
MORIR-to die	MORÍ, moriste, MURIÓ, morimos, murieron
PEDIR-to ask for	PEDÍ, pediste, PIDIÓ, pedimos, pidieron

NOTE that with the exceptions of LEER and CREER, which really are orthographic changes, FEW IRREGULAR PRETERITES CARRY A WRITTEN ACCENT. (Some old books may have accents, but officially the accent was dropped more than 30 years ago.) The verbs QUERER, SABER, and PODER are not frequently used in the preterite. (See Chapter 8) The verbs IR and SER are the same in the preterite. The meaning is made clear by the context of the sentence.

SOME ADVERBIAL PHRASES ASSOCIATED WITH THE PRETERITE

ayer	(yesterday)	anteayer	(the day before yesterday)
anoche	(last night)	la semana pasada	(last week)
ayer a las tres	(yesterday at 3:00)	hace un mes	(a month ago)
el año pasado	(last year)	hace dos años	(two years ago)

7-D FORMATION OF ADVERBS

Many adverbs in English that end in -LY (rapidly) can be formed in Spanish by adding -MENTE to the feminine form of the adjective. If the original adjective has a written accent, it is carried on to the adverb.

rápida-----rápidamente   (rapid---rapidly)   normal---normalmente (normal---normally)

VOCABULARY AND CULTURAL NOTES

a) *de vacaciones* (on vacation)   Estamos de vacaciones. (We are on vacation.) In Spanish a vacation is see as several days and therefore is always used in the plural form. In many countries, besides the summer vacation, people tend not to work during Holy Week (*Semana Santa*) and often they have the week between Christmas and New Year's as well.   One day off is usually called *un día de fiesta* or *un día feriado*.

b) *dominico* (Dominican--of the Dominican Order) *el orden* (order, arrangement) *la orden religiosa* (religious order for men or women) *los dominicos* (Dominican men) *las dominicas* (Dominican sisters) When referring to people from the Dominican Republic, the word is *dominicano/a*.

CHAPTER 8

GOOD FRIDAY

TAPESCRIPT

REFLEXIVES   (8-A)

(Listen and repeat)

Miro el coche.	I look at the car.
Miro el espejo.	I look at the mirror.
ME miro en el espejo.	I look at myself in the mirror.
Miro a Paco en el espejo.	I look at Paco in the mirror.
Lo miro en el espejo.	I look at him in the mirror.
Paco SE mira en el espejo.	Paco looks at himself in the mirror.
(yo) ME llamo...	I call myself [literal] (My name is...)
El SE llama...	He calls himself...
Ella SE llama...	She calls herself...
Ud. SE llama...	You call yourself...
(nosotros) NOS llamamos...	We call ourselves...
Ellos SE llaman...	They call themselves...
Uds. SE llaman...	You (pl.) call yourselves...
lavar----lavarse	to wash----to wash oneself
Lavo el coche.	I wash the car.
ME lavo las manos.	I wash the (my) hands.
Ella SE lava el pelo.	She washes her hair.
Ella lava el pelo de su hija.	She washes her daughter's hair.

COMMON REFLEXIVES WITH PRESENT AND FUTURE TENSE VERBS AND INFINITIVE STRUCTURES

(Listen for comprehension)

(levantarse) Alfonso se levantará temprano.
    Vamos a levantarnos tarde.
(ponerse) Los niños se pondrán la ropa.
    Quiero ponerme el suéter porque tengo frío.
(quitarse) Los hombres se quitarán los sombreros.
    Pienso quitarme el abrigo porque tengo calor.
    Siempre nos quitamos los sombreros en la iglesia.
(sentirse) Me siento enfermo.
    Los pacientes se sentirán mejor mañana.
(divertirse) Me divierto en la fiesta.
    Uds. se divertirán durantes las vacaciones.
    Espero divertirme en Florida.
(preocuparse) Me preocupo por mi familia.
    Susana se preocupa por sus hijos.
    Nos preocuparemos por Uds.
    Ud. no tiene que preocuparse tanto.
(olvidarse) Me olvido de su dirección.
    Nunca nos olvidaremos de Ud.
    Ellos se olvidarán en dos minutos.
    Ud. debe olvidarse del problema.
(aprovecharse) Nos aprovechamos de la oportunidad.
    Quieren aprovechase de las clases de inglés.
(darse cuenta de)
    Me doy cuenta de que Ud. tiene razón.
    Ellos se darán cuenta de que hoy es Viernes Santo.
(preparar---prepararse)
    Mi madre prepara la comida.
    Preparemos la comida mañana.
    La niña se prepara para la primera comunión.
    Nos preparamos para celebrar la misa.
(casar---casarse)
    El cura casa a los novios.
    El cura los casará el sábado.
    Ellos se casarán en octubre.
    Es tradicional casarse en la primavera.

(to get up) Alfonso will get up early.
    We are going to get up late.
(to put on) The children will put on their clothes.
    I want to put on my sweater because I am cold.
(to take off) The men will take off their hats.
    I'm thinking of taking off my coat because I am hot.
    We always take off our hats in church.
(to feel) I feel sick.
    The patients will feel better tomorrow.
(to enjoy oneself) I enjoy myself at the party.
    You will enjoy yourselves on vacation.
    I hope to enjoy myself in Florida.
(to worry oneself) I worry about my family.
    Susan worries about her children.
    We will worry about you (pl.)
    You must not worry so much.
(to forget) I forget his address.
    We will never forget you.
    They will forget in two minutes.
    You ought to forget the problem.
(to take advantage) We take advantage of the opportunity.
    They want to take advantage of the English classes.
(to realize)
    I realize that you are right.
    They will realize that today is Good Friday.
(to prepare---to prepare oneself)
    My mother prepares the meal.
    We will prepare the meal tomorrow.
    The girl prepares herself for her First Communion.
    We are preparing ourselves to celebrate Mass.
(to marry--as a priest   and   to get married--as a couple)
    The priest marries the engaged couple.
    The priest will marry them on Saturday.
    They will get married (to each other) in October.
    It is traditional to get married in the spring.

CARDINAL NUMBERS (by tens and hundreds)   (8-B)

(Listen and repeat)

uno.....diez.....veinte.....treinta	1.....10.....20.....30
cuarenta.....cincuenta.....sesenta	40.....50.....60
setenta.....ochenta.....noventa.....cien	70.....80.....90.....100
ciento uno...ciento dos...ciento tres	101...102...103
doscientos.....trescientos	200.....300
cuatrocientos.....quinientos	400.....500
seiscientos.....setecientos	600.....700
ochocientos.....novecientos	800.....900
mil.....dos mil.....tres mil	1000.....2000.....3000

ORDINAL NUMBERS

primero....segundo....tercero	first....second....third
cuarto....quinto.....sexto.....	fourth....fifth.....sixth
séptimo....octavo....	seventh....eighth
noveno....décimo....	nineth....tenth
la primera vez	the first time
la última vez	the last time
la segunda vez	the second time
el primer piso (el piso primero)	the first floor
el tercer hombre (el hombre tercero)	the third man
el segundo piso (el piso segundo)	the second floor
la Quinta Avenida	Fifth Avenue
el Rey Carlos V (quinto)	King Charles V (the fifth)
el Rey Alfonso X (décimo)	King Alfonso X
el Papa Juan Pablo II (segundo)	Pope John Paul II
el Papa Juan XXIII (veintitrés)	Pope John XXIII (above 10 use cardinal numbers)
el Rey Alfonso XIII (trece)	King Alfonso XIII

ANTES DE // DESPUÉS DE   (8-C)

(Repetición)

Primero trabajamos, DESPUÉS hablamos.
ANTES todo era muy simple.

BEFORE // AFTER

(Repetition)

First we work, afterwards we talk. (adverb)
Before everything was simple.

DESPUÉS todo era muy complicado.	Afterwards everything was complicated.
ANTES DE mi clase	before my class (preposition)
DESPUÉS DEL desayuno	after breakfast
Antes de COMER me lavo las manos.	Before eating I wash my hands.
Como después de LAVARME las manos.	I eat after washing my hands.
Después de levantarse ella se pondrá la ropa.	After getting up she will put on her clothes.
Después de volver ellos se quitarán los abrigos.	After returning they will take off their coats.

IMPERFECT TENSE REVIEW: repeated or on-going action, description in the past, time in the past
(See Chapter 2)

(Listen for comprehension)

Antes siempre (yo) iba al cine.	Before I always used to go to the movies.
Me levantaba tarde porque no trabajaba.	I used to get up late because I wasn't working.
Ud. se levantaba temprano porque trabajaban.	You used to get up early because you (pl.) were working.
Cuando yo era joven veía todas las películas.	When I was young I used to see all the movies.
Nuestra casa era blanca y grande.	Our house was white and large.
Juan era alto y tenía quince años.	John was tall and was 15 years old.
Ellos dormían mucho.	They used to sleep a lot.
Comíamos a las seis.	We used to eat at 6:00.
¿Qué hora era?	What time was it?
--Era la una; eran las dos	It was 1:00; it was 2:00.
Ellos siempre llegaban tarde.	They always used to arrive late.
Los niños recibían muchos regalos.	The children used to receive many gifts.
Era la costumbre poner en libertad a un preso.	It was the custom to free a prisoner.
Los jefes acusaban a Jesús.	The leaders were accusing Jesus.

THE IMPERFECT: mental action

(Listen and repeat)

Pilato quería dar satisfacción al pueblo.	Pilate wanted to give satisfaction to the people.
El romano no quería tener la culpa.	The Roman did not want to be at fault(to have the blame).
Sabía que Jesús no era un criminal peligroso.	He knew that Jesus was not a dangerous criminal.
Ellos creían que Jesús era el rey que esperaban.	They believed that Jesus was the king they awaited.
Pensaban que era injusto crucificarlo.	They thought it was unjust to crucify Him.

"Los jefes de los sacerdotes...querían la muerte de Jesús.	"The head priests wanted Jesus' death.
Buscaban testigos contra él, pero no los encontraban.	They were looking for witness against him but couldn't find any.

En realidad, varios presentaban acusasiones falsas contra él, pero no estaban de acuerdo en lo que decían".

(Marcos 14; 55-56)

In reality, some presented false accusations against him but they couldn't agree over what they were saying".

PRETERITE: Begun or terminated action

(Listen for comprehension)

Entré, me lavé las manos, salí y volví al trabajo.	I entered, washed my hands, left and returned to work.
Marcos entró, se lavó las manos, salió y volvió al trabajo.	Mark entered, washed his hands, left and returned to work.
Entramos, nos lavamos las manos, y salimos.	We entered, we washed our hands, and we left.
Ellos entraron, se lavaron las manos, y salieron.	They entered, washed their hands, and left.
Ayer fui a la tienda y compré un regalo.	Yesterday I went to the store and bought a gift.
Anoche fuimos a la tienda y compramos un regalo.	Last night we went to the store and bought a gift.
El año pasado Uds. fueron allá y compraron un regalo.	Last year you (pl.) went there and bought a gift.
Ellos estudiaron por dos horas.	They studied for two hours.
Anoche los padres comieron a las siete.	Last night the parents ate at 7:00.
Judás vino hacia Jesús y lo besó.	Judas came towards Jesus and kissed Him.
Llevaron a Jesús de Nazaret ante el Sumo Sacerdote.	They took (carried) Jesus of Nazareth before the high priest.
Todos huyeron y abandonaron a Jesús.	They all fled and abandoned Jesus.
Lo torturaron cruelmente en la cruz.	They cruelly tortured Him on the cross.
El Hijo de Dios murió en la cruz.	The Son of God died on the cross.
Dios dio a su único hijo para salvarnos.	God gave his only son to save us.
Cristo redimió al mundo entero.	Christ redeemed the whole world.
Con la muerte de Jesús comenzó una nueva existencia.	With the death of Jesus a new existence began.

THE PRETERITE AND IMPERFECT COMBINED: a rapid or one time action compared to an action or condition in progress

(Listen for comprehension)

Juan llegó mientras comíamos.	John arrived while we we eating.
Ellos caminaban cuando de repente vieron el accidente.	They were walking when suddenly they saw the accident.
Conversábamos cuando ellos llamaron por teléfono.	We were talking when they phoned.
¿Qué hacía ella cuando vio el accidente?	What was she doing when she saw the accident?
--Ella caminaba cuando vio el accicente.	She was walking when she saw the accident.
¿Qué hizo ella cuando vio el accidente?	What did she do when she saw the accident?
--Ella llamó a la policía cuando vio el accidente.	She called the police when she saw the accident.

DIFFERENCES IN MEANING BETWEEN SOME PRETERITE AND IMPERFECT VERBS (8-D)

(Listen and repeat)

(conocer) Conocía a Isabel.	I knew Isabel.
Conocí a Isabel ayer.	I met Isabel yesterday (for the first time).
(saber) Él sabía la respuesta.	He knew the answer.
Yo sabía que era importante.	I knew it was important.
Él supo la verdad.	He found out the truth.
(querer) Ud. quería estudiar.	You wanted to study.
Ana no quería ir.	Ana didn't want to go.
Ud. quiso estudiar.	You tried to study but failed.
Ana no quiso ir.	Ana refused to go.
(poder) Podían hacer el trabajo.	They were able to do the work.
Pudieron hacer el trabajo.	They succeeded in doing the work.
No pudieron hacer el trabajo.	They did not succeed in doing the work.

PRACTICE THE IMPERFECT

(Substitute the imperfect tense for the present tense. The correct answer will follow the pause.)

Carmelita bebe. (*Carmelita bebía.*)   Carmelita drinks. (*Carmelita used to drink.*)

Ellos tienen trabajo. (*Ellos tenían trabajo.*)   They have work. (*They used to have work.*)

Ud. se lava el pelo. (*Ud. se lavaba el pelo.*)   You wash your hair. (*You used to wash your hair.*)

Uds. me dicen algo. (*Uds. me decían algo.*)   You (pl.) tell me something.(*You used to tell me something.*)

Ellos escriben cartas. (*Ellos escribían cartas.*)   They write letters. (*They were writing letters.*)

Paco escucha. (*Paco escuchaba.*)   Paco listens. (*Paco was listening, used to listen.*)

Hago el trabajo. (*Hacía el trabajo.*)   I do the work. (*I was doing the work.*)

Lo compramos. (*Lo comprábamos.*)   We buy it. (*We used to buy it.*)

No comemos mucho. (*No comíamos mucho.*)   We don't eat much. (*We didn't used to eat much.*)

Uds. se ponen los sombreros. (*Uds. se ponían los sombreros.*)   You (pl.) put on your hats. (*You were putting on your hats.*)

Quiero leer. (*Quería leer.*)   I want to read. (*I wanted to read.*)

Ellos saben la respuesta. (*Ellos sabían la respuesta.*)   They know the answer. (*They knew the answer.*)

Ud. puede hablar español. (*Ud. podía hablar español.*)   You can speak Spanish. (*You were able to speak Spanish.*)

Pablo es alto. (*Pablo era alto.*)   Paul is tall. (*Paul was tall.*)

Vamos a misa. (*Íbamos a misa.*)   We go to Mass. (*We were going to Mass.*)

PRACTICE THE PRETERITE

(Substitute the imperfect with *ayer* (yesterday) and the preterite form. The correct answer will follow.)

Antes él estudiaba. Ayer... (*Ayer él estudió.*)
Before he used to study. (*Yesterday he studied.*)

Antes ellos comían. (*Ayer ellos comieron.*)
Before they used to eat. (*Yesterday they ate.*)

Antes el tren llegaba. (*Ayer el tren llegó.*)
Before the train used to arrive. (*Yesterday it arrived.*)

Antes Uds. iban a misa. (*Ayer Uds. fueron a misa.*)
Before you used to go to Mass. (*Yesterday you went to Mass.*)

Antes ellos no compraban nada.
(*Ayer ellos no compraron nada.*)
Before they didn't used to buy anything.
(*Yesterday they didn't buy anything.*)

Antes él ponía el libro en la mesa.
(*Ayer él puso el libro en la mesa.*)
Before he used to put the book on the table.
(*Yesterday he put the book on the table.*)

Siempre ellos volvían a las cinco.
(*Ayer ellos volvieron a las cinco.*)
They always used to return at 5:00.
(*Yesterday they returned at 5:00.*)

Antes él decía algo.
(*Ayer él dijo algo.*)
Before he used to say something.
(*Yesterday he said something.*)

Antes Ud. conocía a Ana.
(*Ayer Ud. conoció a Ana.*)
Before you knew Ana.
(*Yesterday you met Ana.*)

DIRECT OBJECT PRONOUNS AND REFLEXIVES USED TOGETHER (8-A)

(Listen and repeat)

Me pongo el abrigo.---Me lo pongo.
I put on my coat.---I put it on.

La señora se quita el suéter.---La señora se lo quita.
The lady takes off her sweater.--The lady takes it off.

Nos lavamos el pelo.--Nos lo lavamos.
We wash our hair.--We wash it.

Ellos se lavaron el pelo.--Ellos se lo lavaron.
They washed their hair.---They washed it.

Yo no me lavé las manos.---Yo no me las lavé.
I didn't wash my hands.--I didn't wash them.

Espero que Ud. compre el libro.
I hope that you buy the book.

Espero que Ud. lo compre.
I hope that you buy it.

Quiero que ella se lave las manos.
I want her to wash her hands.

Quiero que ella se las lave.
I want her to wash them.

Voy a ponerme el abrigo.
I am going to put on my coat.

Voy a ponérmelo. // Me lo voy a poner.
I am going to put it on (2 ways)

Ella quiere quitarse el suéter.
She wants to take off her sweater.

Ella quiere quitárselo. // Ella se lo quiere quitar.
She wants to take it off. (2 ways)

Queremos lavarnos el pelo.
We want to wash our hair.

Queremos lavárnoslo. // Nos lo queremos lavar.
We want to wash it. (2 ways)

Compre Ud. el libro.---Cómprelo Ud.	Buy the book.---Buy it.
No lo compre Ud.	Don't buy it.
Vean Uds. la película.---Véanla Uds.	See the movie---See it.
No la vean Uds.	Don't see it.
Haga Ud. el trabajo.---Hágalo Ud.	Do the work.---Do it.
No lo haga Ud.	Don't do it.
Póngase Ud. el abrigo.---Póngaselo Ud.	Put on the coat---Put it on.
No se lo ponga Ud.	Don't put it on.
Lávese Ud. las manos.---Láveselas Ud.	Wash you hands.---Wash them.
No se las lave Ud.	Don't wash them.
Quítese Ud. los zapatos.---Quíteselos Ud.	Take off your shoes.--Take them off.
No se los quite Ud.	Don't take them off.

MORE REVIEW OF IMPERFECT AND PRETERITE VERBS

(Answer the questions with the suggested information. The correct answer will follow the pause.)

¿Qué lee la hermana Rosa?   (un libro)
(*La hermana Rosa lee un libro*)

What does Sister Rose read? (a book)
(*Sister Rose reads a book*)

¿Cuándo fueron ellos a la tienda?   (ayer)
(*Ellos fueron a la tienda ayer.*)

When did they go to the store? (yesterday)
(*They went to the store yesterday*)

¿Cuándo regresó el mecánico?   (a la una)
(*El mecánico regresó a la una.*)

When did the mechanic return? (at 1:00)
(*The mechanic returned at 1:00.*)

¿Qué quería hacer Antonio?   (conversar)
(*Antonio quería conversar.*)

What did Antonio want to do (converse)
(*Antonio wanted to converse.*)

¿Cuándo llegó la mujer?   (después de comer)
(*La mujer llegó después de comer.*)

When did the woman arrive? (after eating)
(*The woman arrived after eating.*)

¿Por qué él comió temprano?   (tenía hambre)
(*Él comió temprano porque tenía hambre.*)

Why did he eat early? (he was hungry.)
(*He ate early because he was hungry.*)

¿Por qué bebieron ellos tanto?   (tenían sed)
(*Ellos bebieron tanto poque tenían sed.*)

Why did they drink so much? (they were thirsty)
(*They drank so much because they were thirsty.*)

¿Por qué Ana se puso el suéter?   (tenía frío)

Whey did Ana put on her sweater? (she was cold)

(Ana se puso el suéter porque tenía frío.)	*(Ana put on her sweater because she was cold.)*
¿ Por qué estaba ella en el hospital? (estaba enferma)	Why was she in the hospital? (she was sick)
(Ella estaba en el hospital porque estaba enferma.)	*(She was in the hospital because she was sick.)*
¿Dónde estuvo Carlos ayer? (en la oficina)	Where was Carlos yesterday? (in the office)
(Carlos estuvo en la oficina ayer.)	*Carlos was in the office yesterday.*
¿Quién siempre iba al cine? (Yo)	Who used to always go to the movies? (I)
(Yo siempre iba al cine.)	*(I used to always go to the movies.)*

GRAMMAR

8-A   REFLEXIVE VERBS AND PRONOUNS

Reflexive pronouns are used when the action in the sentence is both executed and received by the subject. Dictionaries distinguish between regular verbs and reflexive verb with SE.

LAVAR--to wash

LAVARSE--to wash oneself

The reflexive pronoun is the same as the direct and indirect object pronouns for *yo, 'tú* and *nosotros* (ME, TE, NOS)
The third person singular and plural are the same: SE.

As with direct and indirect object pronouns, the reflexive pronoun is placed BEFORE THE CONJUGATED VERB.

LAVARSE-to wash oneself   PONERSE-to put on(oneself)   DIVERTIRSE-to enjoy oneself

yo	ME lavo	ME pongo	ME divierto
tú	TE lavas	TE pones	TE diviertes
Ud.	SE lava	SE pone	SE divierte
nosotros	NOS lavamos	NOS ponemos	NOS divertimos
Uds.	SE lavan	SE ponen	SE divierten

With an infinitive or a gerund the reflexive pronoun may be attached or separate and before.

1) Voy a lavar**me**.   (I am going to wash myself.)
   Estoy lavándo**me**.   (I am washing myself.)

2) **Me** voy a lavar.   (I am going to wash myself.)
   Me estoy lavando.   (I am washing myself.)

Direct, indirect and reflexive pronouns MUST BE ATTACHED TO THE AFFIRMATIVE COMMAND.
   Póngase Ud. el abrigo.   (Put on your coat.)
   Levántense Uds.   (Get up.)
However, direct, indirect and reflexive pronouns MUST BE SEPARATE AND BEFORE THE NEGATIVE COMMAND.
   No se ponga Ud. el abrigo. (Don't put on you coat.)
   No se levanten Uds.   (Don't get up.)

When direct objects and reflexive pronouns are used together, the REFLEXIVE ALWAYS IS FIRST.
   Póngaselo Ud. (Put it on--the coat)
   No se lo ponga Ud. (Don't put it on--the coat.)
   (yo) me lo pongo. (I put it on.)
   Voy a ponérmelo.   (I am going to put it on.)

8-B   CARDINAL NUMBERS 100+   (see Chapter 1)

100	cien	101 ciento uno	105 ciento cinco 124 ciento veinticuatro
200	doscientos	doscientos libros (200 books)	doscientas chicas (200 girls)
300	trescientos		
400	cuatrocientos		
500	quinientos		
600	seiscientos		
700	setecientos		
800	ochocientos		
900	novecientos		

1000   mil   2000 dos mil   3000 tres mil
un millón (one million)   dos millones (two million)
1965 Mil novecientos sesenta y cinco
1898 Mil ochocientos noventa y ocho
1492 Mil cuatrocientos noventa y dos

ORDINAL NUMBERS

In Spanish ordinal numbers are used only up to tenth. Eleven and after become cardinal numbers.
primer/o   (see 6-b)   (first)   sexto/a   (sixth)
segundo/a   (second)   séptimo/a (seventh)

tercer/o	(third)	octavo/a	(eighth)
cuarto/a	(fourth)	noveno/a	(ninth)
quinto/a	(fifth)	décimo/a	(tenth)

el primer piso // el piso primero (the first floor)
el primero de enero (January 1--only the first of the month takes an ordinal number)
la quinta calle (the fifth street)
Carlos II (Carlos segundo)
Alfonso X (Alfonso décimo)
Alfonso XI (Alfonso once)

8-C Prepositions in Spanish are often multiple words. Some are directly related to adverbs.
      Antes (Adverb--before)   Antes de (Preposition--before)
      Después (Adverb--afterwards) Después de (Preposition--after)
Any verb following a preposition in Spanish must take the infinitive.
      Antes de comer (before eating)   Después de lavarse (After washing oneself)
      Para comer (In order to eat)   A dormir (To sleep)

8-D VERBS THAT CHANGE MEANING BETWEEN THE IMPERFECT AND PRETERITE

Four commonly used verbs change as follows:
    CONOCER--Imperfect= *knew* over a period of time
         Ellos conocían a Marta durante años. (They knew Marta for years.)
        Preterite=*met* as for the first time
         Ellos conocieron a Marta en la fiesta. (They met Marta at the party.)
    SABER------Imperfect=*knew*
        Sabíamos la respuesta. (We knew the answer.)
       Preterite= *found out*
        Antonio supo la verdad. (Antonio found out the truth.)
    QUERER----Imperfect=*wanted*
        Ellas querían comprar un regalo. (They wanted to buy a gift.)
      Preterite=*tried but failed; refused*
        Ellas quisieron comprar un regalo pero no encontraron nada. (They tried to buy a gift but couldn't
          find anything.)
        Tomás no quiso trabajar. (Tomas refused to work.)
    PODER------Imperfect=*were able*
        Ellos podían ayudarnos. (They were able to help us.)
      Preterite=*succeeded*
        Ellos pudieron ayudarnos. (They succeeded in helping us.)

CHAPTER 9

EASTER

TAPESCRIPT

VOCABULARY RELATED TO EASTER

(Listen and repeat)

Semana Santa	Holy Week
Domingo de Ramos	Palm Sunday
Viernes Santo	Good Friday
la Pascua	Easter
la Resurrección	the Resurrection
la Última Cena	the Last Supper
nacimiento	birth
renacimiento	rebirth
las procesiones religiosas	religious processions
en lugares públicos	in public places
Celebramos la Semana Santa // con procesiones religiosas en lugares públicos.	We celebrate Holy Week // with religious processions in public places.
conquistar---conquistó	to conquer--he conquered
Cristo conquistó la muerte.	Christ conquered death.
esperar---la esperanza	to wait or hope---hope
La resurrección significa	The Resurrection signifies
La resurrección quiere decir que hay esperanza sobre los obstáculos.	The Resurrection means that there is hope over obstacles.
compartir--compartimos	to share--we share
Compartimos su victoria y gloria // sobre la muerte.	We share his victory and glory // over death.

valer la pena--vale la pena	to be worth while--it is worth while
no valer nada--no vale nada	to be worth nothing--it is worthless
El dinero, el poder,	Money, power,
la fama, el placer // no valen nada.	fame, pleasure // are worthless.
la tortura del calvario	the torture of Calvary
Vale la pena // la tortura del calvario.	The torture of Calvary is worth while.
La muerte ha sido conquistada.	Death has been conquered.
volver a nacer	to be born again
volver a preguntar	to ask again
Él volvió a preguntar.	He asked again.
Él preguntó otra vez.	He asked again.
Él preguntó de nuevo.	He asked again.
sufrir--el sufrimiento	to suffer--suffering
identificarse--nos identificamos	to identify oneself with--we identify ourselves
Nos identificamos con el sufrimiento de Cristo.	We identify with Christ's suffering.

PAST PARTICIPLES   (9-A)

(Listen and repeat)

hablar---hablado	to speak--spoken
regresar---regresado	to return---returned
ayudar---ayudado	to help---helped
comer---comido	to eat---eaten
aprender---aprendido	to learn---learned
vivir---vivido	to live---lived
salir---salido	to leave---left
robar---robado	to steal---stolen
el coche robado	the stolen car
cerrar---cerrado	to close---closed
el libro cerrado	the closed book
la ventana cerrada	the closed window
abrir---abierto	to open---opened
El libro está abierto.	The book is open.
La ventana está abierta.	The window is open.
cansar---cansado	to tire--tired
Estamos cansados.	We are tired.
casar---casado	to marry---married
los casados (los esposos)	the married couple, spouses

Ellos son casados.	They are a married couple.
Ellos están casados.	They are married.

PRESENT PERFECT TENSE (9-B)

(Listen and repeat)

(yo) HE hablado	I have spoken
HE comido	I have eaten
He vivido	I have lived
Ud. HA regresado	You have returned
Él HA cerrado	He has closed
Ella HA abierto	She has opened
Uds. HAN pensado	You (pl.) have thought
Ellos HAN mirado	They have watched
Ellas HAN escuchado	They have listened
(nosotros) HEMOS comido	We have eaten
HEMOS salido	We have left (gone out)
HEMOS estado	We have been
HEMOS sido	We have been

UNOS VERBOS IRREGULARES

SOME IRREGULAR VERBS

(Escuche y repita Ud.)

(Listen and repeat)

abrir---ABIERTO	to open---opened
Susana ha abierto la ventana.	Susan has opened the window.
decir---DICHO	to say--said
Uds. han dicho la verdad.	You (pl.) have said the truth.
escribir---ESCRITO	to write---written
Hemos escrito todo el libro.	We have written the whole book.
hacer---HECHO	to make, do---made
Ellos han hecho los sombreros.	They have made the hats.
ir---IDO	to go---gone
He ido a California.	I have been to California.
morir---MUERTO	to die---dead
Cristo ha muerto en la cruz.	Christ has died on the cross.
poner---PUESTO	to put---put
Elena ha puesto el libro en la mesa.	Elena has put the book on the table.

ver---VISTO
Hemos visto la nueva película.
volver---VUELTO
Los Sres. Torres han vuelto a casa.
Un refrán: Dicho y hecho.

to see---seen
We have seen the new movie.
to return---returned
Mr. and Mrs. Torres have returned home.
A saying: No sooner said than done.

(You will be given an infinitive and a subject. Supply the correct form of the present perfect verb.)

conversar---Yo---(*Yo he conversado*)
tener---Carlos---(*Carlos ha tenido*)
creer---nosotros---(*Nosotros hemos creído*)
leer---Ella ---(*Ella ha leído*)
recibir---Ud. ---(*Ud. ha recibido*)
conocer---Yo---(*Yo he conocido*)
saber---Uds.---(*Uds. han sabido*)
llegar---Los padrinos---(*Los padrinos han llegado*)
escoger----Ana y yo---(*Ana y yo hemos escogido*)
ver--Yo---(*Yo he visto*)
lavarse---Él---(*Él se ha lavado*)
prepararse---Yo---(*Yo me he preparado*)
ponerse--Nosotros---(*Nosotros nos hemos puesto*)

to converse---I ---(*I have conversed*)
to have---Carlos---(*Carlos has had*)
to believe---we--(*We have believed*)
to read---She---(*She has read*)
to receive---You---(*You have received*)
to know (people)---I ---(*I have known*)
to know (information)--You--(*You have known*)
to arrive--the godparents--(*The godparents have arrived*)
to chose--Ana and I---(*Ana and I have chosen*)
to see---I---(*I have seen*)
to wash oneself---He---(*He has washed himself*)
to prepare oneself--I---(*I have prepared myself*)
to put (clothing) on---We---(*We have put on*)

(Listen and repeat)

dudar---yo dudo---he dudado
quejarse---yo me quejo---yo me he quejado
rezar---yo rezo---yo he rezado
robar---yo robo---yo he robado
portarse---yo me porto---yo me he portado
cometer---yo cometo---yo he cometido
estafar---yo estafo---yo he estafado

to doubt---I doubt----I have doubted
to complain---I complain---I have complained
to pray---I pray---I have prayed
to rob--I rob---I have robbed
to behave oneself---I behave---I have behaved
to commit---I commit---I have committed
to cheat---I cheat---I have cheated

SOME QUESTIONS TO PREPARE FOR CONFESSION

(For simplicity, answer the questions *in the negative*. The correct answer will follow.)

¿Ha pensado Ud. en los Diez Mandamientos?
(--*No, no he pensado en los Diez Mandamientos.*)
¿Ha dudado Ud. cosas de fe?

Have you thought about the Ten Commandments?
(*No, I haven't thought about the Ten Commandments.*)
Have you doubted articles of faith?

(--*No, no he dudado cosas de fe.*) | (*No, I haven't doubted articles of faith.*)

¿Se ha quejado Ud. de Dios? | Have you complained about God?
(--*No, no me he quejado de Dios*) | (*No, I haven't complained about God.*)
¿Ha rezado Ud.? | Have you prayed?
(--*No, no he rezado.*) | (*No, I haven't prayed.*)
¿Ha ido a misa frecuentemente? | Have you gone to Mass frequently?
(--*No, no he ido a misa frecuentemente.*) | (*No, I haven't gone to Mass regularly.*)
¿Se ha portado bien Ud. con su familia? | Have you behaved well towards your family?
(--*No, no me he portado bien con mi familia.*) | (*No, I haven't behaved well toward my family.*)
¿Ha robado Ud.? | Have you robbed?`
(--*No, no he robado.*) | (*No, I haven't robbed*)

PLUPERFECT TENSE (9-C)

(Listen and repeat)

he mirado-----HABÍA mirado | I have watched-----I had watched
Ud. ha salido----Ud. HABÍA salido | You have gone out---You had gone out
Ellos han regresado---Ellos HABÍAN regresado | They have returned----They had returned
Hemos vuelto-----HABÍAMOS vuelto | We have returned---We had returned
Maribel ha tenido---Maribel HABÍA tenido | Maribel has had---Maribel had had
¿Qué ha hecho el Sr. López? | What has Mr. Lopez done?
--Él no ha hecho nada. | He hasn't done anything
--Él ha puesto el libro aquí. | He has put the book here.
--Él ha escrito la carta. | He has written the letter.
¿Qué HABÍA hecho el Sr. López? | What had Mr. Lopez done?
--Él no HABÍA hecho nada. | He had not done anything.
--Él HABÍA visto la película. | He had seen the movie.
--Él HABÍA ido al restaurante. | He had gone to the restaurant.

(You will hear the present perfect. Give the pluperfect of the same. The correct answer will follow.)

Él ha estudiado. | He has studied.
(*Él había estudiado.*) | (*He had studied.*)
El avión no ha llegado. | The plane has not arrived.
(*El avión no había llegado.*) | (*The plane had not arrived.*)
(Yo) he abierto la ventana. | I have opened the window.
(*Había abierto la ventana.*) | (*I had opened the window.*)
Ellos se han casado. | They have gotten married.

(*Ellos se habían casado.*)
Hemos vuelto de vacaciones.
(*Habíamos vuelto de vacaciones.*)
Ud. no ha escuchado bien.
(*Ud. no había escuchado bien.*)
Hemos hecho el café.
(*Habíamos hecho el café.*)
Ella ha entendido.
(*Ella había entendido.*)
Los Sánchez han vuelto a México.
(*Los Sánchez habían vuelto a México.*)

(*They had gotten married.*)
We have returned from vacation.
(*We had returned from vacation.*)
You haven't listened well.
(*You hadn't listened well.*)
We have made the coffee.
(*We had made the coffee.*)
She has understood.
(*She had understood.*)
Mr. and Mrs. Sanchez have returned to Mexico.
(*Mr. and Mrs. Sanchez had returned to Mexico.*)

HOW TO USE THE PREPOSITIONS PARA// POR (9-D)

(Listen and repeat)

PARA: direction towards, destination, intended for

Las cartas son para ella.
El regalo es para mi hijo.
ropa para damas (mujeres)
ropa para caballeros (hombres)
Me voy para mi pueblo.

The letters are for her.
The gift is for my son.
ladies' clothing
men's clothing
I'm going to my town.

PARA: *in order to*

Para comprar serapes hay que ir a Saltillo.
Para tener soldados hay que ir a Chihuahua.
Necesitamos fe para poder cargar nuestras cruces.

In order to buy serapes (blankets) one must go to Saltillo.
In order to get soldiers one must go to Chihuahua.
We need faith in order to carry our crosses (burdens).

PARA: something to be done within a time limit

Para mañana Uds. deben seleccionar la música.
Para martes tenemos que estudiar la lección.

By tomorrow you (pl.) ought to select the music.
By Tuesday we have to study the lesson.

POR: along, through

Ellos caminan por el parque.
Vamos en coche por la carretera principal.

They walk through the park.
We are going by car along the main highway.

Ud. viaja por México.	You are travelling around (through) Mexico.
Los ladrones entran por la ventana abierta.	The thieves enter through the open window.

POR= durante (during)   The word might be omitted.

Vivieron en Cuba ocho años.	They lived in Cuba 8 years.
Vivieron en Cuba por ocho años.	They lived in Cuba for 8 years.
Vivieron en Cuba durante ocho años.	They lived in Cuba during 8 years.
Estudié (por) seis semanas en la República Dominicana.	I studied (for) 6 weeks in the Dominican Republic.
(yo) Había trabajado por ocho horas.	I had worked for 8 hours.

POR: exchange

Gracias por el regalo.	Thanks for the gift.
(pagar) Cuánto pagó Ud. por el libro?	(to pay) How much did you pay for the book?
Ojo por ojo, diente por diente.	An eye for an eye, a tooth for a tooth.

POR: *for the sake of*

Cristo murió por nosotros.	Christ died for our sake.
Alfonso trabajó por su familia.	Alfonso worked for the sake of his family.
Leonor se sacrificó por sus hijos.	Leonor sacrificed herself for the sake of her children.

MODISMOS--IDIOMATIC PHRASES WITH *POR*

por ejemplo	for example
Sé muchas cosas, por ejemplo, sé manejar un coche.	I know many things, for example, how to drive a car.
por Dios!	for Heaven's sake!
Por Dios! Ayúdame!	For Heaven's sake! Help me!
por eso	for that reason
Ana vive en ese pueblo. Por eso, debe conocerlo.	Ana lives in that town. For that reason she ought to know him.
por favor	please
Por favor, haga Ud. el trabajo rápidamente.	Please, do the work quickly.
por fin	finally
Ellos trabajaron horas y por fin han terminado.	They worked for hours and finally have finished.
por lo general	generally
Por lo general los obreros están aquí temprano.	Generally the workers are here early.
por lo menos	at least
Por lo menos Ud. me ha ayudado.	At least you have helped me.

por medio de	by means of
Nos identificamos con Cristo por medio de nuestra vida de fe, esperanza y caridad.	We identify with Christ by means of our life of faith, hope and charity.
por todas partes	everywhere
Vemos la gloria de Dios por todas partes.	We see the glory of God everywhere.
por la mañana (en la mañana)	in the morning
por la tarde (en la tarde)	in the afternoon
por la noche (en la noche)	in the evening
Los estudiantes leían por la mañana.	The students used to read in the morning.
Ellos tenían clases por la tarde.	They used to have classes in the afternoon.
Ellos salían con sus amigos por la noche.	They used to go out with their friends in the evening.

EL CONVENTO DE MOUNT SAINT MARY

(Repita Ud. el vocabulario nuevo)

el edificio	the building
impresionante	impressive
está situado	it is located
la región	the region
los árboles	the trees
las colinas	the hills
el río	the river
fundar--fundaron	to found--founded
crecer--creció	to grow--it grew
la orden religiosa	the religious order
organizar---organizó	to organize--organized
una parte del trabajo	a part of the work
hoy día	today, nowadays
la biblioteca	the library
el teatro	the theater
el gimnacio	the gymnasium
las residencias	the residences, dormitories
la escuela primaria (elemental)	the elementary school
además	besides
orgulloso	proud
oír--oyen	to hear--they hear
la estatua	the statue
el altar mayor	the main altar

a la derecha	to the right
a la izquierda	to the left
las vidrieras	stained glass windows
diaria, diariamente	daily
el mármol	marble

LISTENING COMPREHENSION

El convento de las hermanas dominicas de Mount Saint Mary es un edificio impresionante con vista del Río Hudson. Está situado en Newburgh, Nueva York, a unas cincuenta millas hacia el norte de Manhattan. La región es muy bonita, con árboles, flores y colinas.

En 1883 las monjas fundaron el convento con la misión de enseñar a chicas. Creció el convento y la orden religiosa organizó un colegio (escuela) para jóvenes. La enseñanza siempre ha sido una parte del trabajo de las dominicas. Hoy día, gracias a la dedicación y visión de estas hermanas católicas, además de un convento, hay una universidad de 1200 estudiantes con biblioteca, teatro, gimnacio, residencias y una escuela primaria (elemental).

Las monjas son orgullosas de la capilla de estilo neogótico donde oyen misa diaria. El altar mayor es de mármol. A la izquierda está una estatua de Santa Rosa de Lima y a la derecha está una estatua de Santa Catarina de Siena. Las vidrieras son de muchos colores, por ejemplo, el rojo azul, amarillo y verde que cuentan la vida de la Virgen María, Jesús predicando y la muerte de San José. El interés de estas dominicas en la comunidad hispana no es nuevo. Desde hace años esta orden tiene el Colegio de San José en Villa Caparra, Puerto Rico.

The convent of the Dominican Sisters of Mount Saint Mary is an impressive building with a view of the Hudson River. It is located in Newburgh, New York, about 50 miles north of Manhattan. The region is very pretty with trees, flowers and hills.

In 1883 the nuns founded the convent with the mission to teach girls. The convent grew and the religious order organized a boarding school for young women. Teaching has always been part of the work of Dominican Sisters. Today, thanks to the dedication and vision of these Catholic Sisters, besides a convent, there is a university of 1,200 students with a library, a theater, a gym, dormitories, and an elementary school.

The nuns are proud of the neo-Gothic style chapel where they hear Mass daily. The main altar is made of marble. To the left is a statue of St. Rose of Lima and to the right is a statue of St. Catherine of Siena. The stained glass windows are of many colors, for example, red, blue, yellow and green that tell of the life of the Virgin, Jesus preaching and the death of St. Joseph. The interest of these Dominican Sisters for the Hispanic Community is not new. For years the order has run the the School of St. Joseph in Villa Caparra, Puerto Rico.

GRAMMAR

9-A PAST PARTICIPLES

To form the past participle, add -ADO or -IDO to the infinitive root: HABLAR---HABLADO (spoken)

COMER----COMIDO   (eaten)

VIVIR------VIVIDO   (lived)

COMMON IRREGULAR PAST PARTICIPLES
:

ABRIR (to open)	ABIERTO	ESCRIBIR (to write)	ESCRITO
VER (to see)	VISTO	DECIR (to say)	DICHO
PONER (to put)	PUESTO	HACER (to make, do)	HECHO
VOLVER (to return)	VUELTO	IR (to go)	IDO
MORIR (to die)	MUERTO		

USES OF PAST PARTICIPLES

1) noun   Él es casado. (He is a married man.)
2) adjective   El libro está abierto. (The book is open.)
3) compound verb   He estado aquí antes. (I have been here before.)
4) adjective--with passive voice (see Chapter 11) El libro fue escrito por Cervantes. (The book was written by Cervantes.)

9-B PRESENT PERFECT TENSE

This tense is formed by using the present tense of the auxiliary verb HABER and the past participle.

	HABLAR	COMER	VIVIR	PONERSE	
yo	he hablado	he comido	he vivido	me he puesto	(I have spoken, eaten, lived and put on)
tú	has hablado	has comido	has vivido	te has puesto	(You([fam.] have spoken, eaten, lived, put on)
Ud.	ha hablado	ha comido	ha vivido	se ha puesto	(You have spoken, eaten, lived, put on)
nosotros	hemos hablado	hemos comido	hemos vivido	nos hemos puesto	(We have spoken, eaten, lived, put on)
Uds.	han hablado	han comido	han vivido	se han puesto	(You [pl.] have spoken, eaten, lived, put on)

As seen in the example above of PONERSE, indirect, direct and reflexive pronouns are placed BEFORE the conjugated form of HABER.

9-C PLUPERFECT TENSE

This tense is formed by using the imperfect tense of the auxiliary verb HABER with the past participle meaning *had done*.

	HABLAR	COMER	VIVIR	PONERSE	
yo	había hablado	había comido	había vivido	me había puesto	(I had spoken, eaten, lived, put on)
tú	habías hablado	habías comido	habías vivido	te habías puesto	(You [fam.] had spoken, eaten, lived, put on)
Ud.	había hablado	había comido	había vivido	se había puesto	(You had spoken, eaten, lived, put on)
nosotros	habíamos hablado	habíamos comido	habíamos vivido	nos habíamos puesto	(We had spoken, eaten, lived, put on)
Uds.	habían hablado	habían comido	habían vivido	se habían puesto	(You [pl.] had spoken, eaten, lived, put on)

The preterite perfect, future perfect and conditional perfect are less frequently used and will not be covered in this program.

9-D PARA---POR

Often these prepositions translate as *for* in English. They are, however, not interchangeable and have specific uses in Spanish. The most common uses and meanings are:

PARA 1) direction towards, destination, intended for
       2) *in order to*
       3) something to be done *for* or by a stated time in the future

POR 1) *along* or *through*
      2) *for* or *during* time in past
      3) exchange--one thing *for* another
      4) *for the sake of*
      5) phrases listed in text

CHAPTER 10

CHRISTMAS EVE

TAPESCRIPT

REVIEW OF PRETERITE TENSE   (Listen and repeat)

(comprar) Ayer Ud. compró-- Uds. compraron
(usar)   Ayer él usó--- ellos usaron
(beber) Anoche ella bebió--- ellas bebieron
(comprender) Anoche Ud. comprendió---Uds. comprendieron
(recibir) El año pasado él recibió---ellos recibieron

(to buy) Yesterday you bought---You (pl.) bought
(to use)   Yesterday he used---They used
(to drink) Last night she drank---they drank
(to understand) Last night you understood--You (pl.) understood
(to receive) Last year he received---they received

(After hearing the infinitive and the Ud. form, supply the preterite of Uds. The correct answer will follow.)

(desear) Ud. deseó---(*Uds. desearon*)
(comenzar) Ud. comenzó---(*Uds. comenzaron*)
(dejar) Ud. dejó---(*Uds. dejaron*)
(salir) Ud. salió---(*Uds. salieron*)
(regresar) Ud. regresó---(*Uds. regresaron*)
(volver) Ud. volvió---(*Uds. volvieron*)
(asistir) Ud. asistió---(*Uds. asistieron*)
(pensar) Ud. pensó---(*Uds. pensaron*)
(escribir) Ud. escribió---(*Uds. escribieron*)
(conocer) Ud. conoció---(*Uds. conocieron*)
(ver) Ud. vio---(*Uds. vieron*)
(practicar) Ud. practicó---(*Uds. practicaron*)
(arreglar) Ud. arregló---(*Uds. arreglaron*)
(tener) Ud. tuvo---(*Uds. tuvieron*)
(ser) Ud. fue---(*Uds. fueron*)
(lavarse) Ud. se lavó---(*Uds. se lavaron*)

(to wish) You wished---(*You (pl.) wished*)
(to begin) You began---(*You began*)
(to leave-something) You left---(*You left*)
(to leave a place) You left---(*You left*)
(to return) You returned---(*You returned*)
(to return) You returned---(*You returned*)
(to attend) You attended---(*You attended*)
(to think) You thought---(*You thought*)
(to write) You wrote---(*You wrote*)
(to know) You met---(*You met*) (see Chapter 7)
(to see) You saw---(*You saw*)
(to practice) You practiced---(*You practiced*)
(to arrange) You arranged---(*You arranged*)
(to have) You had---(*You had*)
(to be) You were---(*You were*)
(to wash oneself) You washed yourself--(*You washed yourselves*)

Chapter 10 - CHRISTMAS EVE

(ponerse) Ud. se puso---(*Uds. se pusieron*)   (to put on) You put on---(*You put on yourselves*)
(decir) Ud. dijo---(*Uds. dijeron*)   (to say) You said---(*You said*)
(venir) Ud. vino---(*Uds. vinieron*)   (to come) You came---(*You came*)

IMPERFECT SUBJUNCTIVE (10-A)

(Listen and repeat)

Ud. trabaja. Quiero que Ud. trabaje.   You work. I want you to work.
Ud. lo escribe. Prefiero que Ud. lo escriba.   You write it. I prefer that you write it.
Ud. lo tiene. Dudo que Ud. lo tenga.   You have it. I doubt that you have it.
Ud. viene. Es importante que Ud. venga.   You come. It is important that you come.
Ud. se lo pone. Espero que Ud. se lo ponga.   You put it on. I hope that you put it on.
Ud. está aquí. Siento mucho que Ud. no esté aquí.   You are here. I am very sorry that you are not here.

(trabajar) Quiero que Ud. trabaje.   (to work) I want you to work.
    Quería que Ud. TRABAJARA. (10-A)   I wanted you to work.
    Quise que Ud. TRABAJARA.   I wanted (but failed) to get you to work.
(comer) Prefiero que Ud. coma.   (to eat) I prefer that you eat.
    Prefería que Ud. COMIERA.   I was preferring that you eat.
    Preferí que Ud. COMIERA.   I preferred that you eat.
(escribirlo) Espero que Ud. lo escriba.   (to write it) I hope that you write it.
    Esperaba que Ud. lo ESCRIBIERA.   I was hoping that you would write it.
    Esperé que Ud. lo ESCRIBIERA.   I hoped that you would write it.
(decir) Es importante que Ud. diga algo.   (to say) It is important for you to say something.
    Era importante que Ud. DIJERA algo.   It was important for you to say something.
    Fue importante que Ud. DIJERA algo.   It was important for you to say something.
(venir) Ojalá que Ud. venga. (10-a)   (to come) Would that you come.
    Ojalá que Ud. VINIERA.   Would that you would come.
(lavarse) Es dudoso que Ud. se lave.   (to wash oneself) It is doubtful that you wash yourself.
    Era dudoso que Ud. se LAVARA.   It was doubtful that you washed yourself.
    Fue dudoso que Ud. se LAVARA.   It was doubtful that you washed yourself.
(ponerse) Es lástima que Ud. se ponga el sombrero.   (to put on yourself) It is a shame that you put on your hat.
    Era lástima que Ud. se PUSIERA el sombrero.   It was a shame that you put on your hat.
    Fue lástima que Ud. se PUSIERA el sombrero.   It was a shame that you put on your hat.

Carlos esperaba que yo VINIERA.   Carlos was hoping that I would come.
Carlos esperaba que Ud. VINIERA.   Carlos was hoping that you would come.
Carlos esperaba que Elena VINIERA.   Carlos was hoping that Elena would come.

Carlos esperaba que nosotros VINIÉRAMOS.	Carlos was hoping that we would come.
Carlos esperaba que Uds. VINIERAN.	Carlos was hoping that you (pl.) would come.
Carlos esperaba que ellos VINIERAN.	Carlos was hoping that they would come.
Ellos dudaron que yo ESTUVIERA aquí.	They doubted that I was here.
Ellos dudaron que Ud. ESTUVIERA aquí.	They doubted that you were here.
Ellos dudaron que Elena ESTUVIERA aquí.	They doubted that Elena was here.
Ellos dudaron que nosotros ESTUVIÉRAMOS aquí.	They doubted that we were here.
Ellos dudaron que Uds. ESTUVIERAN aquí.	They doubted that you (pl.) were here.

(You will hear an infinitive and the present subjunctive form. Give the imperfect subjunctive form. The answer will follow.)

ayudar---que ayude---(que ayudara)	to help--may he (she or you) help---(might he help)
hablar---que hable---(que hablara)	to speak---may he speak---(might he speak)
beber---que beba---(que bebiera)	to drink---may he drink---(might he drink)
asistir---que asista---(que asistiera)	to attend---may he attend---(might he attend)
tener---que tenga---(que tuviera)	to have---may he have---(might he have)
dar---que dé---(que diera)	to give---may he give---(might he give)
salir---que salga---(que saliera)	to leave---may he leave---(might he leave)
estar---que esté---(que estuviera)	to be---may he be---(might he be)
ser---que sea---(que fuera)	to be---may he be---(might he be)
hacer---que haga---(que hiciera)	to make or do---may he do---(might he do)
vivir---que viva---(que viviera)	to live---may he live---(might he live)
conversar---que converse---(que conversara)	to converse---may he converse---(might he converse)
saber---que sepa---(que supiera)	to know---may he know---(might he know)
conocer---que conozca---(que conociera)	to know (people)---may he know---(might he know)
levantarse---que se levante---(que se levantara)	to get up---may he get (himself) up---(might he get up)
ponerse---que se ponga---(que se pusiera)	to put on oneself---may he put on---(might he put on)
decirlo---que lo diga---(que lo dijera)	to say it---may he say it---(might he say it)
querer---que quiera---(que quisiera)	to want---may he want---(might he want)

CONDITIONAL TENSE   (10-B)

(Listen and repeat)

regresar---regresaría	to return---would return
comer---comería	to eat---would eat
recibir---recibiría	to receive---would receive
yo regresaría	I would return

Ud. regresaría	You would return
Nosotros regresaríamos	We would return

decir---Ud. diría---Uds. dirían	to say---you would say---you (pl.) would say
hacer---Ud. haría---Uds. harían	to make, do---you would do---" would do
querer---Ud. querría---Uds. querrían	to want---you would want---you (pl.) would want
poder--Ud. podría---Uds. podrían	to be able--you would be able---" would be able
saber---Ud. sabría---Uds. sabrían	to know---you would know--- " would know
poner--Ud. pondría---Uds. pondrían	to put---you would put--- " would put
ponerse---Ud. se pondría---Uds. se pondrían	to put on--you would put on--- " would put on
tener--Ud. tendría---Uds. tendrían	to have---you would have--- you (pl.) would have
venir---Ud. vendría---Uds. vendrían	to come---you would come--- " would come
salir---Ud. saldría---Uds. saldrían	to leave---you would leave--- " would leave

INDIRECT DISCOURSE WITH FUTURE AND CONDITIONAL VERBS (10-C)

(Listen and repeat)

Ellos dicen que vendrán en coche.	They say they will come by (in) car.
Ellos dijeron que VENDRÍAN en coche.	They said they would come by car.
Pedro dice que trabajará los sábados.	Pedro says he will work on Saturdays.
Pedro dijo que TRABAJARÍA los sábados.	Pedro said he would work on Saturdays.
Los niños dicen que no tendrán miedo.	The children say they will not be afraid.
Los niños dijeron que no TENDRÍAN miedo.	The children said they would not be afraid.
Decimos que ellos llegarán pronto.	We say that they will arrive soon.
Dijimos que ellos LLEGARÍAN pronto.	We said that they would arrive soon.

CONTRARY TO FACT PHRASES WITH THE IMPERFECT SUBJUNCTIVE AND CONDITIONAL (10-D)

(Listen and repeat)

No soy presidente, pero si yo FUERA presidente...	I am not the president, but if I were the president...
No soy Ud., pero si yo FUERA Ud...	I am not you, but if I were you...
Pedro no tiene dinero, pero si él TUVIERA dinero...	Pedro doesn't have money, but if he had money...
Ellos no están aquí, pero si ellos ESTUVIERAN aquí...	They are not here, but if they were here...
Ud. no lo sabe, pero si Ud. lo SUPIERA...	You don't know it, but if you knew it...
¿Qué haría Luisa si ella fuera presidenta?	What would Luisa do if she were president?
Si Luisa fuera presidenta, ¿qué haría ella?	If Luisa were president, what would she do?
--Si Luisa fuera presidenta, ella ayudaría a todos.	If Luisa were president, she would help everyone.

Si yo fuera Ud., (yo) escucharía las cintas a menudo.	If I were you, I would listen to the tapes often.
Si yo fuera Ud., (yo) descansaría un poco.	If I were you, I would rest a bit.
Si yo fuera Elena, (yo) me casaría con Pedro.	If I were Elena, I would marry Pedro.
Si él tuviera el dinero, compraría un coche.	If he had the money, he would buy a car.
Si tuviéramos el dinero, compraríamos regalos.	If we had the money, we would buy gifts.
Si ellos estuvieran aquí, nos darían el dinero.	If they were here, they would give us the money.
Si Ud. lo supiera, estaría enojado.	If you knew it, you would be angry.
Si no tuviera que trabajar, él iría a misa.	If he didn't have to work, he would go to Mass.

(Answer the questions by making the infinitive phrase conditional. The correct answer will follow.)

Si Pepe tuviera unas vacaciones, ¿qué haría él?	If Pepe had a vacation, what would he do?
visitar a sus padres	to visit his parents
(*Si Pepe tuviera unas vacaciones, él visitaría a sus padres.*)	(*If Pepe had a vacation, he would visit his parents*)
Si Ud. tuviera unas vacaciones, ¿adónde iría Ud.?	If you had a vacation, where would you go?
ir a México	to go to Mexico
(*Si yo tuviera unas vacaciones, iría a México.*)	(*If I had a vacation, I would go to Mexico.*)
Si ellos tuvieran más dinero, ¿qué comprarían?	If they had more money, what would you buy?
comprar ropa	to buy clothing
(*Si ellos tuvieran más dinero, comprarían ropa.*)	(*If they had more money, they would buy clothing.*)
Si estuviera Rambo, ¿qué haría él?	If Rambo were here, what would he do?
salvarnos	to save us
(*Si Rambo estuviera, nos salvaría.*)	(*If Rambo were here, he would save us.*)
Si Ud. fuera doctora, ¿qué haría Ud.?	If you were the doctor, what would you do?
darle la medicina	to give him(her) the medicine
(*Si yo fuera doctora, le daría la medicina.*)	(*If I were the doctor, I would give him (her) the medicine.*)
Si la hermana no comprendiera español, ¿qué haría ella?	If the sister didn't understand Spanish, what would she do?
escuchar las cintas muchas veces	to listen to the tapes often
(*Si la hermana no comprendiera español, ella escucharía las cintas muchas veces.*)	(*If the sister did not understand Spanish, she would listen to the tapes often.*)

SOME CHRISTMAS VOCABULARY
(Listen and repeat)

la Navidad	Christmas
La Navidad es el veniticinco de diciembre.	Christmas is December 25.
la Nochebuena	Christmas Eve
La Nochebuena es la noche del veinticuatro de diciembre.	Christmas Eve is the night of December 24.
la Misa de Gallo	Christmas Eve Mass

Después de la Misa de Gallo muchas familias hispanas regresan a casa para una cena especial.	After Christmas Eve Mass, many Hispanic families return home for a special dinner.
el día de Reyes (los Reyes Magos)	Epiphany, Day of the Three Kings
El día de Reyes es el seis de enero.	The Three Kings Day is January 6.
Los niños recibían regalos el 6 de enero.	The children used to receive gifts of January 6.
La influencia norteamericana cambia unas tradiciones.	American influence changes some traditions.
el árbol de Navidad	the Christmas tree
los regalos para Navidad	Christmas gifts
el Nacimiento	the Nativity scene
las estatuas de la Virgen María, San José y el Niño	the statues of the Virgin Mary, St. Joseph and the Christ Child
los pastores y las ovejas	the shepherds and the sheep
los reyes y los camellos	the Kings and the camels
los villancicos	Christmas carols
los aguinaldos puertorriqueños	Puerto Rican carols
La Navidad es el nacimiento del Niño Jesús.	Christmas is the birth of the Baby Jesus.

NOCHE DE PAZ   (SILENT NIGHT)

Noche de Paz, Noche de amor,	Night of Peace, Night of love,
todo duerme en derredor	all around is sleeping
entre los astros que esparcen su luz	Between the stars is scattered light
bella anunciando al Niño Jesús	announcing to the Christ Child
Brilla la estrella de paz,	Shines the star of peace,
Brilla la estrella de paz.	" " " "

ADESTE FIDELES   (COME ALL YE FAITHFUL)

Venid, fieles todos	Come, all ye faithful
a Belén marchemos;	let us march to Bethlehem;
alegres, triunfantes y	happy, triumphant and
llenos de amor.	full of love.
Cristo ha nacido,	Christ has been born,
Cristo Rey Divino.	Christ the Divine King.
Venid, adoremos,	Come, let us adore (Him)
Venid, adoremos	" " " "
Venid, adoremos	" " " "
a nuestro Señor.	our Lord.

LA IGLESIA DE SAN PATRICIO	THE CHURCH OF ST. PATRICK
(Escuche y repita Ud. el vocabulario nuevo)	(Listen and repeat the new vocabulary)

los inmigrantes irlandeses	the Irish immigrants
el comercio	commerce
la parroquia	the parish
los feligreses	the parishioners
bilingüe	bilingual
hispanoparlantes	Spanish-speakers
los representantes	the representatives
rico--enriquecer	rich--to enrich
buscar	to look (for)
últimamente	lately

(Escuche Ud. para comprender)

(Listen to undertand)

La iglesia de San Patricio en Newburgh fue fundada por inmigrantes irlandeses hace 156 años. Durante muchos años las fábricas y el comercio del Río Hudson atraían a muchos italianos e irlandeses al pueblo y a la parroquia. Desde hace treinta años hay también muchos feligreses hispanos y ahora San Patricio es una iglesia bilingüe.
Los primeros hispanoparlantes que llegaron eran puertorriqueños pero ahora hay representantes de trece países hispanoamericanos. Hay muchos de Centroamérica que buscan la libertad y el trabajo. Últimamente hay muchos "poblanos", mexicanos del Estado de Puebla. Los hispanos enriquecen la parroquia con sus tradiciones, su energía y su música. Hay misa en inglés y en español. Los problemas a veces son diferentes pero todos adoran a Cristo Nuestro Señor.
"Que todos sean uno..."
(Juan 17; 21)

The Church of St. Patrick in Newburgh was founded by Irish immigrants 156 years ago. During many years the factories and the commerce of the Hudson River attracted many Italians and Irish to the town and the parish. For thirty years there have been many Hispanic parishioners, and now St. Patrick's is a bilingual church.

The first Spanish-speakers were Puerto Ricans but now there are representatives from thirteen Spanish American countries. There are many from Central America who look for freedom and work. Lately there are many "poblanos", Mexicans from the State of Puebla. The Hispanics enrich the parish with their traditions, their energy and their music. There are Masses in English and Spanish. Sometimes the problems are different but all worship Christ Our Lord.
"May they all be one..."
(John 17; 21)

¿COMPRENDE UD.? (Answer *cierto* or *falso* to the statements given. If *falso*, the correction follows.)

1) La iglesia es de Santo Tomás. (10-b)
   (FALSO--La iglesia es de San Patricio.)

The church is of St. Thomas.
(FALSE-The church is of St. Patrick.)

2) Fundaron la iglesia hace 156 años.
   (CIERTO)

It was founded 156 years ago.
(TRUE)

3) La parroquia tenía muchos inmigrantes italianos
e irlandeses. (10-c)
   (CIERTO)

The parish used to have many Italian and Irish
immigrants.
(TRUE)

4) Los hispanoparlantes son personas que hablan francés.
(FALSO--Los hispanoparlantes hablan español.)

"Hispanoparlantes" are people who speak French.
(FALSE--"Hispanoparlantes speak Spanish.)

5) Ahora hay muchos feligreses del Caribe, la América
Central y México.
   (CIERTO)

Now there are parishioners from the Caribbean, Central
America and Mexico.
(TRUE)

GRAMMAR

10-A   IMPERFECT SUBJUNCTIVE

The third person plural of the preterite is the root for the imperfect subjunctive. To this root are added the personal endings -ARA,-ARAS,-ARA,-ÁRAMOS, -ARAN to -AR verbs and -IERA, -IERAS,-IERA, -IÉRAMOS,-IERAN to -ER and -IR verbs. A second set of endings (--ase//--iese), are more literary rather than conversational and will not be used in PASTORAL SPANISH.

	HABLAR (hablaron)	COMER (comieron)	VIVIR (vivieron)
yo	hablara	comiera	viviera
tú	hablaras	comieras	vivieras
Ud.	hablara	comiera	viviera
nosotros	habláramos	comiéramos	viviéramos
Uds.	hablaran	comieran	vivieran

REVIEW OF IRREGULAR PRETERITES

	PRETERITE	IMPERFECT SUBJUNCTIVE
ESTAR (to be)	estuvieron	estuviera
TENER (to have)	tuvieron	tuviera
PODER (to be able)	pudieron	pudiera
SABER (to know)	supieron	supiera
PONER (to put)	pusieron	pusiera
HACER (to do, make)	hicieron	hiciera
QUERER (to want)	quisieron	quisiera
VENIR (to come)	vinieron	viniera
DECIR (to say)	dijeron	dijera
LEER (to read)	leyeron	leyera
CREER (to believe)	creyeron	creyera
IR // SER (to go/to be)	fueron	fuera
SENTIR (to feel)	sintieron	sintiera
MORIR (to die)	murieron	muriera
DORMIR (to sleep)	durmieron	durmiera
PEDIR (to ask for)	pidieron	pidiera

The IMPERFECT SUBJUNCTIVE is used in those cases where the subjunctive is required but the verb of the main clause is in the imperfect, preterite or conditional tense.

PRESENT SUBJUNCTIVE:
Quiero que Ud. **haga** el trabajo.   (I want you to do the work.)
Esperamos que ellos **vengan.**   (We hope that they come.)
Dudan que yo **esté** aquí.   (They doubt that I am here.)
Es posible que **compremos** algo.   (It is possible that we will buy something.)

IMPERFECT SUBJUNCTIVE:
Quería que Ud. **hiciera** el trabajo.   (I wanted you to do the work.)
Esperábamos que ellos **vinieran.**   (We hoped that they would come.)
Dudaron que yo **estuviera** aquí.   (They doubted that I was here.)
Era posible/ sería posible que **compráramos** algo. (It was/would be possible that we would buy something.)

10-B CONDITIONAL TENSE

Just as the future tense, (see Chapter 4), the conditional tense is formed by adding one set of personal endings to the entire infinitive. It translates as *would do something.*

	HABLAR	COMER	VIVIR	
yo	hablaría	comería	viviría	(I would speak, eat, live)
tú	hablarías	comerías	vivierías	(You [fam.] would speak, eat, live)
Ud.	hablaría	comería	viviría	(You would speak, eat, live)
nosotros	hablaríamos	comeríamos	viviríamos	(We would speak, eat, live)
Uds.	hablarían	comerían	vivirían	(You [pl.] would speak, eat, live)

The same verbs are irregular in the future and the conditional.

DECIR	diría	HACER	haría
QUERER	querría	PODER	podría
SABER	sabría	SALIR	saldría
PONER	pondría	TENER	tendría
VENIR	vendría		

10-C INDIRECT DISCOURSE WITH FUTURE AND CONDITIONAL VERBS

Present-----Future
Ellos dicen que **vendrán.**
(They say they will come.)

Past-------Conditional
Ellos dijeron que **vendrían.**
(They said they would come.)

10-D CONTRARY TO FACT WITH IMPERFECT SUBJUNCTIVE AND CONDITIONAL

SI YO FUERA... (If I were..) Must be subjunctive because it is IMPOSSIBLE. The verb after *si* (if) (10-d) is the IMPERFECT SUBJUNCTIVE. The verb in the main clause is in the CONDITIONAL tense.

Si yo FUERA Ud., COMPRARÍA un carro.   (If I were you, I would buy a car.)
COMPRARÍA un carro si yo FUERA Ud.   (I would buy a car if I were you.)

Si TUVIÉRAMOS el dinero no TRABAJARÍAMOS.   (If we had the money, we wouldn't work.)
No TRABAJARÍAMOS si TUVIÉRAMOS el dinero.   (We wouldn't work if we had the money.)

VOCABULARY AND CULTURAL NOTES

a) *Ojalá* (God grant it so, would that it be) The word can be used independently. *Ojalá que* always takes the subjunctive. This is an example of the Arabic influence on the Spanish language, *Alá,* meaning God.

b) *San* (Saint) Before a woman's name it is always *Santa,* as *Santa Ana, Santa Teresa.*
San is usually the form before a man's name, as *San Francisco, San Antonio.* However, if the saint's name begins with DO or TO , the word *santo* is used as in *Santo Tomas, Santo Domingo.* This change is to avoid the confusion of *un San Tomás=santo más* (one more saint rather than St. Thomas).

c) *e* (and) When the word after the conjunction begins with *i* or *hi* (silent *h*) *e* is used instead of the normal *y* to distinguish the sounds. For example, the usual conjunction is *y* as *libros y sillas* (books and chairs).
Examples with *e* are: *italianos e ingleses* (Italians and Englishmen) or *francés e historia* (French and history).
Likewise, *u* replaces the conjunction *o* (or). *Estudiar o salir* (to study or to leave) is most common, but to avoid the repetition of *o, u* is used as in *días u horas* (days or hours) or *ellos u otros* (they or others).

d) *si* (if) or *sí* (yes) The written accent here does not change the sound but indicates a different part of speech. Other examples of this are: *él* (he) and *el* (the); interrogative words ¿*qué?* (what) and *que* (that); *tú* (you-familiar) and *tu* (your); *mi* (my) and *mí* (object of the preposition-to me).

CHAPTER 11

CHRISTMAS

TAPESCRIPT

FORMING GERUNDS (PRESENT PARTICIPLES)   (11-A)

(Listen and repeat)

hablar---hablando	to speak---speaking
alabar---alabando	to praise---praising
practicar---practicando	to practice---practicing
comer---comiendo	to eat---eating
beber---bebiendo	to drink---drinking
escribir---escribiendo	to write---writing
salir---saliendo	to leave---leaving

(Give the gerund after hearing the infinitive. The correct answer will follow.)

dejar---(dejando)	to leave---(leaving)
volver---(volviendo)	to return---(returning)
glorificar--(glorificando)	to glorify---(glorifying)
pensar---(pensando)	to think---(thinking)
vivir---(viviendo)	to live---(living)
manejar---(manejando)	to drive or manage---(driving)
hacer---(haciendo)	to make or do---(doing)
conocer--(conociendo)	to know (people)---(knowing)

saber---(sabiendo)	to know (information)---knowing
recordar---(recordando)	to remember---(remembering)

SOME IRREGULAR GERUNDS

(Listen and repeat)

leer--leyendo	to read---reading
creer---creyendo	to believe---believing
decir---diciendo	to say---saying
pedir---pidiendo	to ask for---asking for
dormir---durmiendo	to sleep---sleeping
morir---muriendo	to die---dying
sentir---sintiendo	to feel---feeling

THE PRESENT TENSE AND THE PROGRESSIVE TENSES   (11-B)

(Listen and repeat)

Hoy (yo) hablo con Uds.	Today I speak (am speaking) with you (pl.)
En este momento...	At this moment...
Ahora mismo...	Right now...
En este momento (yo) estoy hablando con Uds.	At this moment I am speaking with you.
Ahora mismo estoy hablando con Uds.	Right now I am speaking with you.
Escucho la música.	I listen to the music.
Ahora mismo estoy escuchando la música.	Right now I am listening to the music.
Bebo el vino.	I drink the wine.
Ahora mismo estoy bebiendo el vino.	Right now I am drinking the wine.
Recibo un regalo.	I receive a gift.
Ahora mismo estoy recibiendo un regalo.	Right now I am receiving a gift.
Leo la homilía.	I read the homily.
Estoy leyendo la homilía.	I am reading the homily.
Pido perdón.	I ask for forgiveness.
Estoy pidiendo perdón.	I am asking for forgiveness.
Pienso en mi familia.	I think about my family.
Estoy pensando en mi familia.	I am thinking about my family.
Vuelvo a casa.	I return home.
Estoy volviendo a casa.	I am returning home.

(After hearing the present tense, give the present progressive form of the verb. The correct answer will follow.)

Hablo por teléfono.
(*Estoy hablando por teléfono.*)
Miro la televisión.
(*Estoy mirando la televisión.*)
Dejo un recado.
(*Estoy dejando un recado.*)
Comienzo el trabajo.
(*Estoy comenzando el trabajo.*)
Recuerdo el número.
(*Estoy recordando el número.*)
Manejo el carro.
(*Estoy manejando el carro.*)
Leo el correo.
(*Estoy leyendo el correo.*)
Digo la verdad.
(*Estoy diciendo la verdad.*)

I speak on the phone.
(*I am speaking on the phone.*)
I watch television.
(*I am watching television.*)
I leave a message.
(*I am leaving a message.*)
I begin the work.
(*I am beginning the work.*)
I remember the number.
(*I am remembering the number.*)
I drive the car.
(*I am driving the car.*)
I read the mail.
(*I am reading the mail.*)
I say the truth.
(*I am saying the truth.*)

(Listen and repeat)

Estoy hablando con Ud.
Ud. está hablando conmigo.
Alicia está hablando conmigo.
Fernando está hablando con nosotros.
Uds. están cantando.
Ellos están cantando también.
Nosostros estamos cantando.
Uds. y yo no estamos cantando.

I am speaking with you.
You are speaking with me.
Alicia is speaking with me.
Fernando is speaking with us.
You (pl.) are singing.
They are also singing.
We are singing.
You (pl.) and I not are singing.

(After hearing the present tense verb, give the present progressive form. The answer will follow.)

La feligresa escucha.
(*La feligresa está escuchando.*)
Ellos firman el documento.
(*Ellos están firmando el documento.*)
El cura predica.
(*El cura está predicando.*)
Ellos celebran la misa.

The parishioner listens.
(*The parishioner is listening.*)
They sign the document.
(*They are signing the document.*)
The priest preaches.
(*The priest is preaching.*)
They celebrate Mass.

(Ellos están celebrando la misa.)
Nosotros leemos el Antiguo Testamento.
(Nosotros estamos leyendo el Antiguo Testamento.)
Aprendemos el mensaje del evangelio.
(Estamos aprendiendo el mensaje del evangelio.)

(They are celebrating Mass.)
We read the Old Testament.
(We are reading the Old Testament.)
We learn the message of the Gospel.
(We are learning the message of the Gospel.)

(Listen and repeat)

Estoy practicando obras de caridad.
Estoy practicándolas.
Estamos glorificando el nombre de Dios.
Estamos glorificándolo.
Estoy obedeciendo los mandamientos.
Estoy obedeciéndolos.
Estamos protegiendo a los niños.
Estamos protegiéndolos.
Dios está dirigiéndonos.
Dios nos está dirigiendo.
El pastor está guardando las ovejas.
El pastor está guardándolas.
El pastor las está guardando.
Ellos están mirándose en el espejo.
Ellos se están mirando en el espejo.
Estoy lavándome las manos.
Estoy lavándomelas.
Me las estoy lavando.
Ellos están lavándose el pelo.
Ellos están lavándoselo.
Ellos se lo están lavando.
Me siento en la silla.
Estoy sentándome en la silla.
Me estoy sentando en la silla.

I am practicing charitable works.
I am practicing them.
We are glorifying the name of God.
We are glorifying Him.
I am obeying the Commandments.
I am obeying them.
We are protecting the children.
We are protecting them.
God is directing us.
God is directing us.
The shepherd is guarding the sheep.
The shepherd is guarding them.
The shepherd is guarding them.
They are looking at themselves in the mirror.
They are looking at themselves in the mirror.
I am washing my hands.
I am washing them.
I am washing them.
They are washing their hair.
They are washing it.
They are washing it.
I sit (myself) on the chair.
I am sitting down on (in) the chair.
I am sitting down on the chair.

PRESENT AND IMPERFECT PROGRESSIVE TENSES (11-C)

(Listen and repeat)

Estoy hablando por teléfono.
Estaba hablando por teléfono.

I am speaking on the phone.
I was speaking on the phone.

La abuela está ayudándonos.	The grandmother is helping us.
La abuela estaba ayudándonos.	The grandmother was helping us.
Ellos están leyendo el evangelio.	They are reading the Gospel.
Ellos estaban leyendo el evangelio.	They were reading the Gospel.
Nosotros estamos protegiéndonos.	We are protecting ourselves.
Nosotros estábamos protegiéndonos.	We were protecting ourselves.
Nosotros nos estábamos protegiendo.	We were protecting ourselves.

(After hearing the present progressive form of the verb, supply the imperfect progressive form. The answer will follow.)

La hermana Silvia está enseñando.	Sister Sylvia is teaching.
(La hermana Silvia estaba enseñando.)	*(Sister Sylvia was teaching.)*
Los niños están durmiendo.	The children are sleeping.
(Los niños estaban durmiendo.)	*(The children were sleeping.)*
Dios nos está guiando.	God is guiding us.
(Dios nos estaba guiando.)	*(God was guiding us.)*
Estamos recibiendo las cenizas.	We are receiving the ashes.
(Estábamos recibiendo las cenizas.)	*(We were receiving the ashes.)*
El abuelito está muriendo.	The grandfather is dying.
(El abuelito estaba muriendo.)	*(The grandfather was dying.)*
Nos estamos lavando las manos.	We are washing our hands.
(Nos estábamos lavando las manos.)	*(We were washing our hands.)*

OTHER USES OF GERUNDS (11-D)

(Listen and repeat)

continuar---yo continúo---Ud. continúa	to continue---I continue---You continue
seguir---yo sigo---Ud. sigue	to continue---I continue---You continue
Yo continúo cantando.	I continue to sing (singing)
La tía continúa escuchando la radio.	The aunt continues listening to the radio.
Sigo estudiando con cuidado.	I continue studying with care (carefully).
El mecánico sigue trabajando con cuidado.	The mechanic continues working carefully.
Los jóvenes siguen leyendo cuidadosamente.	The youths continue reading carefully.
Las muchachas salen de la escuela corriendo.	The girls leave the school running.
Dejé a los estudiantes hablando de la política.	I left the students talking about politics.
Lo hallaron en el templo haciendo preguntas.	They saw him in the temple asking questions.
Los pastores se fueron alabando a Dios.	The shepherds went away praising the Lord.

PASTORAL SPANISH

SOME USES OF THE INFINITIVE INSTEAD OF THE GERUND

(Listen and repeat)

Después de comer	After eating
Después de levantarse	After getting (oneself) up
Antes de volver	Before returning
Antes de sentarme, hablo con la secretaria.	Before sitting (myself), I speak to the secretary.
Me gusta caminar por el parque.	I like walking (to walk) through the part.
A José le gustaba ir al cine.	Jose used to like going (to go) to the movies.
Al salir de la casa	Upon leaving the house
Al llegar a la iglesia	Upon arriving at the church
Carlos entró en la casa sin saludar a su madre.	Carlos entered the house without greeting his mother.
Ellos hablaron sin pensar.	They spoke without thinking.

EL NACIMIENTO DEL NIÑO JESÚS / THE BIRTH OF THE CHRIST CHILD

(Escuche y repita Ud. el vocabulario nuevo)

(Listen and repeat the new vocabulary)

la buena nueva	the Good News
la alegría, la felicidad	happiness
el ángel, los ángeles	the angel, the angels
el cielo	the sky, heaven
la tierra	the earth
el acontecimiento	the event, the happening
el corazón	the heart
el rebaño de ovejas	the flock of sheep
hallar	to find
un recién nacido	a newborn child
el primogénito	the first-born son
pañales	swaddling clothes ("diapers" in modern Spanish)
les produjo un miedo	made them fearful
no teman	do not be afraid

"Cuando estaban en Belén,	"When they were in Bethlehem,
le llegó el día	there arrived the day
en que María debía tener su hijo.	that Mary was to have her child.
Y dio a luz su primogénito,	And she gave birth to her first-born son,
she wrapped lo envolvió en pañales	she wrapped him in swaddling clothes

y lo acostó en una pesebrera,
porque no había lugar para ellos
en la sala común.

En la región había pastores
que vivían en el campo
y que por la noche se turnaban
para cuidar sus rebaños.
El ángel del Señor se les apareció
y los rodeó de claridad la Gloria del Señor,
y todo esto les produjo un miedo enorme.

Pero el ángel les dijo:
 No teman, porque yo vengo a comunicarles
una buena nueva que será motivo de alegría
para todo el pueblo.
Hoy ha nacido para ustedes
en la ciudad de David un Salvador
que es Cristo Señor.
En esto lo reconocerán:
hallarán a un niño recién nacido
envuelto en pañales y acostado en una pesebrera.
De pronto aparecieron otros ángeles
y todos alababan a Dios,
diciendo: Gloria a Dios en lo más alto del cielo,
y en la tierra, gracia y paz a los hombres.

...Fueron...y hallaron a María, José y al recién nacido...
María, por su parte, observaba cuidadosamente
todos estos acontecimientos
y los guardaba en su corazón.

Después los pastores se fueron
glorificando y alabando a Dios
porque todo lo que habían visto y oído
era tal como se lo habían anunciado."

and she lay him in a manger,
because there was no space for them
in the inn (the main room.)

In the region there were shepherds
that lived in the country(side)
and by night took turns
in order to take care of the flocks.
The Angel of the Lord appeared to them
and the glory of the Lord shone around them,
and all this made them fearful.

But the angel told them:
Do not fear, because I come to tell you
good news which will bring happiness
to all the people.
Today is born for you
in the City of David a Savior
who is Christ the Lord.
This is how you will recognize him:
You will find a new-born child
wrapped in swaddling clothes lying in a manger.
Suddenly there appeared other angels
and all were praising God,
saying, Glory to God in the highest of heaven,
and on earth, grace and peace to all mankind.

...They went... and found Mary, Joseph and the newborn child...
Mary carefully was observing
all these events
and keeping them in her heart.

Afterwards the shepherds left
Glorifying and praising God,
because all that they had seen and heard
was just as it had been foretold."

(Luke 2; 6-21)

SOME EXAMPLES OF THE PASSIVE VOICE (11-E)

(Listen and repeat)

(Voz activa) Cervantes escribe la novela.
(Voz pasiva) La novela ES ESCRITA por Cervantes.
    El libro ES ESCRITO por Cervantes.
    Los libros SON ESCRITOS por Cervantes.
(Voz activa) El ladrón roba el dinero.
(Voz pasiva) El dinero ES ROBADO por el ladrón.
    Las bolsas SON ROBADAS por el ladrón.
(Voz activa) El terremoto destruyó la ciudad.
(Voz pasiva) La ciudad FUE DESTRUÍDA por el terremoto.
(Voz activa) La criada preparó un plato.
(Voz pasiva) El plato FUE PREPARADO por la criada.
    Los platos FUERON PREPARADOS por la criada.
    Las comidas FUERON PREPARADAS por la criada.

(Active voice) Cervantes writes the novel.
(Passive voice) The novel is written by Cervantes.
    The book is written by Cervantes.
    The books are written by Cervantes.
(Active voice) The thief steals the money.
(Passive voice) The money is stolen by the thief.
    The handbags are stolen by the thief.
(Active voice) The earthquake destroyed the city.
(Passive voice) The city was destroyed by the earthquake.
(Active voice) The maid prepared a dish.
(Passive voice) The dish was prepared by the maid.
    The dishes were prepared by the maid.
    The meals were prepared by the maid.

THE PASSIVE VOICE WITH *SE* (11-F)

(Listen and repeat)

Aquí se habla español.
Se dice que él está enfermo.
Se abre la tienda a las nueve de la mañana.
Se cierra la oficina a las siete.
Se vende ropa para mujeres aquí.
Se venden corbatas en esta tienda.
Se compran muchas cosas en el mercado.
Se abren las tiendas muy temprano.
Se hacen coches en esa fábrica (factoría)

Spanish is spoken here.
It is said that he is sick.
The store is opened at 9:00 in the morning.
The office is closed at 7:00.
Clothing for women is sold here.
Ties are sold in this store.
Many things are bought in the market.
The stores are opened early.
Cars are made in that factory.

VOCABULARY BUILDING

(Listen and repeat)

el libro--un objeto
librero--una persona que vende libros
librería--una tienda que vende libros

book--an object
book seller
bookstore

---

el pan	bread
panadero--una persona que hace pan	baker
panadería--una tienda que vende pan	bakery
la carne	meat
carnicero--una persona que vende carne	butcher
carnicería--una tienda que vende carne	butcher shop
entrar---la entrada	to enter---the entrance
salir---la salida	to leave---the exit (also departures)
llegar---la llegada	to arrive---the arrival
pensar--el pensamiento--un niño pensativo	to think--the thought--a pensive child
enseñar--la enseñanza	to teach--the teaching(s)
esperar--la esperanza	to wait or hope--hope
aconsejar--el consejo--el consejero	to advise--advise--advisor (person)
cuidar-- Cuidado!--con cuidado--cuidadosamente	to take care of--Be careful!--with care--carefully
comer--la comida--el comedor--comilón	to eat--the meal--the diningroom--glutton
cocinar--la cocina--el cocinero--el cocido	to cook--kitchen--cook--a type of stew

GRAMMAR

11-A FORMING GERUNDS

Gerunds, also known as present participles, are formed from the infinitive. The -AR verbs take --ANDO and others take --IENDO.

hablar	hablando	(speaking)
comer	comiendo	(eating)
vivir	viviendo	(living)

There are relatively few irregular verbs but some that have been used in the text are:

decir	diciendo	(saying)
pedir	pidiendo	(asking for)
sentir	sintiendo	(feeling)
venir	viniendo	(coming)
dormir	durmiendo	(sleeping)
morir	muriendo	(dying)

Some irregular forms are due to spelling rather than pronunciation changes.

creer	creyendo	(believing)
leer	leyendo	(reading)

11-B THE PRESENT PROGRESSIVE TENSE

In Spanish the progressive tenses (present and imperfect) emphasize the action in a given moment. Phrases such as *ahora mismo* (right now) and *en este momento* (at this moment) often introduce the progressive. **It is far less common in Spanish than in English.** The auxiliary verb most commonly used is ESTAR, but verbs such as SEGUIR, CONTINUAR may be used.

HABLAR	COMER	VIVIR	
estoy hablando	estoy comiendo	estoy viviendo	(I am speaking, eating, living)
estás hablando	estás comiendo	estás viviendo	(You [familiar] are speaking, eating, living)
está hablando	está comiendo	está viviendo	(He, she or you are speaking, eating, living)
estamos hablando	estamos comiendo	estamos viviendo	(We are speaking, eating, living)
están hablando	están comiendo	están viviendo	(They, You [pl.] are speaking, eating, living)

As with the infinitive, there are two ways to use refelexives and object pronouns with the gerund or present participle.

   1) Attached: Ellos están lavándose. (They are washing themselves.)
                Estoy comprándolos.   (I am buying them.)
   2) Separate and before the conjugated verb: Ellos se están lavando. (They are washing themselves.)
                                         Los estoy comprando.   (I am buying them.)

11-C IMPERFECT PROGRESSIVE TENSE

This tense is parallel to the present progressive tense, but here the verb ESTAR is conjugated in the imperfect form.

PENSAR	APRENDER	DORMIR	
estaba pensando	estaba aprendiendo	estaba durmiendo	(I was thinking, learning, sleeping)
estabas pensando	estabas aprendiendo	estabas durmiendo	(You [fam.] were thinking, learning, sleeping)
estaba pensando	estaba aprendiendo	estaba durmiendo	(He, she, you were thinking, learning, sleeping)
estábamos pensando	estábamos aprendiendo	estábamos durmiendo	(We were thinking, learning, sleeping)
estaban pensando	estaban aprendiendo	estaban durmiendo	(You [pl.] were thinking, learning, sleeping)

The progressive tenses are never used with the verbs IR or VENIR.

11-D SPECIAL INFORMATION ABOUT GERUNDS

The gerund or present participle can be used in a adverbial phrase:

   Lo hallaron en el templo **haciendo** preguntas. (They found him in the temple asking questions.)
   Los niños salieron **cantando.**   (The children left singing.)

However, there are uses of the gerund in English that do not ocur in Spanish. **The infinitive always follows a preposition in Spanish** and the phrase *I like* with nouns will also use infinitives rather than the gerund.

Después de **hablar,** salgo del edificio.   (After speaking, I leave the room.)
Antes de **comer,** nos lavamos las manos.   (Before eating, we wash our hands.)
A María le gusta **caminar.**   (Maria likes walking [to walk].)

11-E   THE PASSIVE VOICE

The passive voice is less commonly used in Spanish than in English. The *true passive* is formed by using SER plus the PAST PARTICIPLE. The agent or person who performed the action is preceded by POR. The past participle agrees with the subject.

El libro es escrito por Cervantes.   (The book is written by Cervantes.)
El libro fue escrito por Cervantes.   (The book was written by Cervantes.)
Las bolsas fueron robadas por el ladrón.   (The handbags were stolen by the thief.)

11-F   A common way to form the passive voice in Spanish is by using the reflexive pronoun *SE* with the third person singular or plural of the verb. This structure is used when the agent who performs the action is unimportant or unknown.

Aquí se vende ropa. (Clothing is sold here.)   Aquí se venden corbatas. (Ties are sold here.)

APPENDIX

SOME INFORMATION ABOUT SPANISH PRONUNCIATION

VOWEL SOUNDS   (This section is on Tape 12 side B)

A   Pronounced like *a* in *father:* casa   Santa Ana   nada   mañana   gracias   habla   trabaja   blanca

E   Pronounced like *a* in *pay:* negro   elegante   elefante   enorme   teléfono   bebé

I   Like *i* in *machine:* cinco   biblia   hijo   días   niño   Cristo   iglesia   librería   difícil

O   Like *o* in *obey:* coco   como   vivo   ocho   esposo   hospital

U   Like *oo* in *boot:* pluma   muchacho   azul   Cuba   Hugo   universidad   cruz   número   cura

SOME CONSONANTS THAT CAUSE CONFUSION FOR ENGLISH-SPEAKERS:

H   The only silent letter in Spanish: hermano   historia   hotel   ahora   Honduras   hay

CH   Pronounced as *ch* in *cheese:* chocolate   chico   mucho   muchacha

L   Like *l* in *lion:* lava   lápiz   libro   él   los

LL   In Latin America like *y* in *yellow* or *j* in *jelly:* me llamo   calle   botella   tortilla   ella   amarillo

N   Like *n* in *nine:* nada   no   nueve   comen   nuevo

Ñ   Like *ni* in *onion:* año   español   España   señor   señorita   piñata

R   Pronounced with a single tap of the tongue: pero   hablar   comer   caro

RR   Written as a double letter it is trilled, also trilled is the initial *r:* perro   carro   Roberto   restaurante   ropa   rosas   rojo

J   Like *h* in *hat:* junio   julio   jueves   Jorge   Jesús

138

GE/ GI Like *h* in *hat:* general inteligente agente Argentina agencia gitano

QUE/ QUI Like *k* in *kite:* que ¿por qué? pequeño queso mosquito aquí quiero ¿quién? quince

STRESSING THE CORRECT SYLLABLE IN SPANISH

Most words in Spanish do not have a written accent mark. The largest number of words in the language have the natural (unwritten) accent on the SECOND TO THE LAST SYLLABLE. These words END with VOWELS, N or S. This group includes most plurals and verbs. Examples are:

casa casas libro libros nombre nombres fecha nacimiento hablan hablamos hablo sacerdote evangelio farmacia

Words that end in a CONSONANT (other than N or S) have the natural (unwritten) accent on the LAST SYLLABLE. Almost all infinitives are in this group.

verdad lugar azul señor hospital profesor mejor universidad sociedad tomar comer conversar escribir español

A small number of words that use the accent to distinguish parts of speech (*el él, ¿qué? que*). However, most words with a written accent need the stress on the syllable with the written accent. Some words at first are quite difficult but with practice can be mastered. Once you understand the stress system, it will be easier to converse and to read Spanish homilies aloud.

inglés francés café fácil fáciles teléfono José tomó yo tomé tomaré tomaría suéter difícil música política número

Jesús lápiz lápices después día María librería recoría sábado miércoles perdón Pérez Sánchez González

ADDITIONAL EXERCISES TO PRACTICE GRAMMAR

(Some exercises are recorded on Tape 12 after the Mass, side B)

SINGULAR AND PLURAL PHRASES

la casa blanca----las casas blancas	the white house---the white houses
el señor simpático----los señores simpáticos	the nice man---the nice men
la vela amarilla----las velas amarillas	the yellow candle---the yellow candles
el coche nuevo----los coches nuevos	the new car---the new cars
el teléfono pequeño----los teléfonos pequeños	the small telephone--the small telephones

la familia grande----las familias grandes   the big family---the big families
la clase fácil----las clases fáciles   the easy class---the easy classes
el amigo sincero----los amigos sinceros   the sincere friend---the sincere friends
el documento importante----los documentos importantes   the important document---the important documents
el cura mexicano---los curas mexicanos   the Mexican priest---the Mexican priests
la conversación interesante----las conversaciones interesantes   the interesting conversation---the interesting conversations

la lección difícil----las lecciones difíciles   the difficult lesson---the difficult lessons
la canción popular----las canciones populares   the popular song---the popular songs
la oración larga----las oraciones largas   the long prayer---the long prayers
la confesión sincera----las confesiones sinceras   the sincere confession---the sincere confessions

la responsabilidad----las responsabilidades   responsibility---responsibilites
la sociedad moderna----las sociedades modernas   modern society---modern societies
la comunidad cristiana----las comunidades cristianas   Christian community---Christian communities
la universidad católica----las universidades católicas   Catholic university---Catholic universities

PRACTICE WITH NUMBERS

La abuela tiene 80 años. (ochenta)   The grandmother is 80 years old.
El niño tiene 8 años. (ocho)   The child is eight.
El señor tiene 46 años. (cuarenta y seis)   The man is 46.
El padrino tiene 50 años. (cincuenta)   The godfather is 50.
La madrina tiene 35 años. (treinta y cinco)   The godmother is 35.
Tengo 19 años. (diecinueve)   I am 19.
Tengo 62 años. (sesenta y dos)   I am 62.

Hoy es el 8 de marzo (ocho)   Today is March 8.
Mañana es el 9 de marzo. (nueve)   Tomorrow is March 9.
La niña nació el 18 de enero. (dieciocho)   The child was born on January 18.
El niño nació el 24 de abril. (veniticuatro)   The child was born on April 24.
El Día de Independencia   Independence Day
El Día de Independencia en México es el 16 de septiembre. (dieciséis)   Independence Day in Mexico is September 16.

El Día de Independencia en los Estados Unidos es el 4 de julio. (cuatro)   Independence Day in the U.S. is July 4.

Tengo 20 libros. (veinte)   I have 20 books.
Tengo 17 velas blancas. (diecisiete)   I have 17 white candles.
Tengo 6 hermanos. (seis)   I have 6 brothers (and sisters).

La iglesia tiene 7 sacramentos. (siete)	The Church has 7 sacraments.
Tenemos 10 Mandamientos. (diez)	We have Ten Commandments.
La oficina tiene 12 teléfonos. (doce)	The office has 12 phones.
La señora tiene 15 vestidos. (quince)	The lady has 15 dresses.
El padre católico tiene 4 biblias. (cuatro)	The Catholic priest has 4 Bibles.

THE FAMILY AND RELATIONS (Chapters 1 and 2)

TÍA Mi tía es la hermana de mi madre.
    Mi tía es la esposa de mi tío.
    Mi tía Inés es amable.
PRIMO Mi primo es el hijo de mis tíos.
    Mi primo Alfonso es de Colombia.
ABUELA Mi abuela nació en San Francisco.
    Mi madre es la hija de mi abuela.
    Mi abuela es la esposa de mi abuelo.
HERMANO Tengo dos hermanos.
    Mi hermano es el padre de mis sobrinos.
    El hermano de mi madre es mi tío.

AUNT My aunt is the sister of my mother.
    My aunt is the wife of my uncle.
    My Aunt Ines is nice.
COUSIN My cousin is the son of my aunt and uncle.
    My cousin Alfonso is from Colombia.
GRANDMOTHER My grandmother was born in San Francisco.
    My mother is the daughter of my grandmother.
    My grandmother is the wife of my grandfather.
BROTHER I have two brothers.
    My brother is the father of my nephews and nieces.
    The brother of my mother is my uncle.

PRACTICE WITH NEGATIONS (Chapter 2)

Quiero el correo.	I want the mail.
No quiero el correo.	I don't want the mail.
Nuestro sacerdote quiere helado.	Our priest wants ice cream.
Nuestro sacerdote no quiere helado.	Our priest doesn't want ice cream.
Mi hermano quiere algo.	My brother wants something.
Mi hermano no quiere nada.	My brother doesn't want anything.
Quiero algo.	I want something.
Nada quiero.	I don't want anything.
No quiero nada.	I don't want anything.
Siempre quiero café.	I always want coffee.
Nunca quiero café.	I never want coffee.
No quiero café nunca.	I never want coffee.

PASTORAL SPANISH

Siempre queremos trabajar.
Nunca queremos trabajar.
No queremos trabajar nunca.

We always want to work.
We never want to work.
We never want to work.

Alguien habla por teléfono.
Nadie habla por teléfono.
No habla nadie por teléfono.
Quiero hablar con alguien.
No quiero hablar con nadie.

Someone is speaking on the phone.
Nobody is speaking on the phone.
Nobody is speaking on the phone.
I want to speak with someone.
I don't want to speak with anyone.

Siempre alguien está en la oficina.
Nunca está nadie en la oficina.
No está nadie nunca en la oficina.

Somebody is always in the office.
Nobody is ever in the office.
Nobody is ever in the office.

Sé algo de (los) coches.
No sé nada de (los) coches.

I know something about cars.
I don't know anything about cars.

¿Sabe Ud. algo de historia?
--No, no sé nada de historia.
¿Sabe Ud. algo de música?
--No, no sé nada de música.

Do you know anything about history?
No, I don't know anything about history.
Do you know anything about music?
No, I don't know anything about music.

PRESENT TENSE VERBS

El señor habla español.
En mi casa hablamos inglés.
El señor García enseña literatura.
Ellos escuchan las cintas.
Miramos la película española.
Las señoras compran en el mercado.
Invitamos a muchos amigos.
Descanso un poquito.
Trabajo mucho todos los días.
El cura explica la situación.
Nuestros amigos pagan en el restaurante.
Las niñas preparan las lecciones.
Los muchachos esperan el tren.
Escucha la música clásica.
Escuchamos a la profesora.

The man speaks Spanish.
In my house we speak English.
Mr. Garcia teaches literature.
They listen to the tapes.
We watch (look at) the Spanish movie.
The women buy (shop) in the market.
We invite many friends. (Note the use of the personal a.)
I rest a bit. (diminutive of the adverb *poco* is *poquito*)
I work a lot every day.
The priest explains the situation.
Our friends pay in the restaurant.
The girls prepare the lessons.
The boys wait for the train.
He (she) listens to classical music.
We listen to the professor. (personal a)

Miro la televisión.	I watch television.
Ellos miran al profesor de inglés.	They look at (watch) the professor of English. (personal **a**)
Necesito un diccionario.	I need a dictionary.
Ellos necesitan hablar con María.	They need to speak with Maria.
Siempre ayudamos a los pobres.	We always help the poor. (personal **a**)
Tomo un café con mis amigos.	I drink coffee with my friends.
Ellos conversan mucho	They converse a lot.
El abuelo firma el documento.	The grandfather signs the document.
Hablamos por teléfono los domingos.	We speak on the phone on Sundays.
aprender--No aprendo los verbos muy bien.	to learn--I don't learn the verbs very well.
creer--Creo que Dios es justo.	to believe--I believe God is just.
comprender--Ud. comprende el problema.	to understand--You understand the problem.
leer--Ellos leen la biblia todos los días.	to read--They read the Bible every day.
vender--Las señoras venden fruta en el mercado.	to sell--The women sell fruit in the market.
beber--Bebemos un refresco.	to drink--We drink a soft drink.
comer--La familia come a las siete.	to eat--The family eats at seven.
ver--Vemos muchas cosas.	to see--We see many things.
escribir--Escribo una carta.	to write--I write a letter.
recibir--Ellos reciben el correo.	to receive--They receive the mail.
vivir--Vivimos en Nueva York.	to live--We live in New York.
salir--Antonio sale temprano.	to leave--Antonio lives early.
conocer--No conozco a los padrinos.	to know (people)--I don't know the godparents.
Ellos conocen a Carolina.	They know Carolina.
Conocemos a muchos cubanos.	We know many Cubans.
saber--No sé nada.	to know--I don't know anything.
Sabemos algo importante.	We know something important.
Ud. sabe que Carlos vive en Colorado.	You know that Carlos lives in Colorado.
Ellos saben la respuesta.	They know the answer.
Marta sabe que el documento es importante.	Marta knows that the document is important.
No sabemos manejar.	We do not know how to drive.
querer--Quiero escoger la música.	to want--I want to choose the music.
Quisiera escoger la música.	I would like to choose the music.
Él quiere recibir una sorpresa.	He wants to receive (get) a surprise.
Él quisiera recibir una sorpresa.	He would like to receive a surprise.
Ud. quiere comer ahora.	You want to eat now.
Ud. quisiera comer ahora.	You would like to eat now.

tener que/ deber	must or have to/ ought to or should
Tengo que descansar.	I have to (must) rest.
Debo (de) descansar.	I ought to (should) rest.
Ellos tienen que preparar la comida.	They have to prepare the meal.
Ellos deben preparar la comida.	They ought to prepare the meal.
Tenemos que buscar a los niños.	We must look for the children.
Debemos buscar a los niños.	We should look for the children.
pensar--Pienso en mi hermano.	to think--I think about my brother.
Ud. piensa salir a las cinco.	You consider (think about) leaving at 5:00.
Ellos piensan que la iglesia es muy bonita.	They think that the church is very beatiful.
Pensamos comer a la una y media.	We are thinking of eating at 1:30.
jugar--Carlitos juega al fútbol.	to play (games)--Carlitos plays soccer.
No juego al tenis.	I don't play tennis.
Ella y yo jugamos en el parque.	She and I play in the park.
recordar--Recuerdo toda la lección.	to remember--I remember the whole lesson.
Ud. recuerda la canción.	You remember the song.
No recordamos los verbos irregulares.	We do not remember the irregular verbs.
entender--Entiendo las palabras nuevas.	to understand--I understand the new words.
Ella no entiende al profesor.	She does not understand the professor.
Él y yo entendemos el problema.	He and I understand the problem.
volver--Vuelvo a las diez.	to return (to a place)--I (will) return at 10:00.
El niño vuelve a casa muy tarde.	The child returns home very late.
Volvemos en la primavera.	We (will) return in the spring.
venir--Vengo a clase tarde.	to come--I come to class late.
El profesor viene temprano.	The professor comes early.
Uds. vienen a las dos en punto.	You (pl.) come at 2:00 on the dot.
ir--Voy a la tienda cada día.	to go--I go to the store each day.
Ud. va a la iglesia muchas veces.	You go to church often.
Vamos a la rectoría cada semana.	We go to the rectory eary week.
Ellos van al hospital una vez al año.	They go to the hospital once a year.
La señora Pérez va al mercado la próxima semana.	Mrs. Perez goes to the market next week.

EXERCISES COMPARING THE PRESENT AND IMPERFECT TENSES (Chapter 2)

Estudio---Antes siempre estudiaba	I study---I always used to study
Hago el café---Antes siempre hacía el café	I make coffee---I always used to make coffee
Vivo---Antes siempre vivía	I live---I always used to live
Trabajo---Antes siempre trabajaba	I work---I always used to work
Digo algo---Antes siempre decía algo	I say something---I always used to say something

Vengo---Antes siempre venía | I come---I always used to come
Veo---Antes siempre veía | I see---I always used to see
Voy---Antes siempre iba | I go---I always used to go
Soy---Antes siempre era | I am---I always used to be
Doy---Antes siempre daba | I give---I used to always give
Estoy---Antes siempre estaba | I was---I always was
Ud. cree---Ud. creía | You believe---You used to believe
Ud. quiere---Ud. quería | You want---You wanted (used to want)
Ella pone---ella ponía | She puts---she used to put (was putting)
Ella escribe---ella escribía | She writes---she used to write
Ud. espera---Ud. esperaba | You wait (or hope)---You used to wait or hope
Ud. canta---Ud. cantaba | You sing---You used to sing
Él tiene---él tenía | He has---He used to have
Él hace---él hacía | He makes (or does)---He used to make
Maribel vuelve---Maribel volvía | Maribel returns---Maribel used to return

Estamos---estábamos | We are---We used to be (were)
escuchamos---escuchábamos | We listen---We used to listen (watch the accent in the -AR verbs)
Nos lavamos---Nos lavábamos | We wash ourselves---We used to wash ourselves
Nos ponemos---Nos poníamos | We put on---We used to put on
comemos---comíamos | We eat--We used to eat
escribimos---escribíamos | We write---We used to write
somos---éramos | We are---We used to be
vamos---íbamos | We go---We used to go

EXCERCISES WITH THE PRESENT SUBJUNCTIVE (Chapter 6)

Quiero ayudar. | I want to help.
Quiero que Ud... | I want you (The following verb must be in the subjunctive form.)
Quiero que Ud. ayude. | I want you to help.
Quiero que ellos ayuden. | I want them to help.
Quiero tomar. | I want to take (eat, drink)
Quiero que ella tome. | I want her to take.
Quiero que ellas tomen. | I want them to take.
Quiero comer. | I want to eat.
Quiero que él coma. | I want him to eat.
Quiero que ellos coman. | I want them to eat.
Quiero salir. | I want to leave.
Quiero que Paco salga. | I want Paco to leave.

PASTORAL SPANISH

Quiero que Paco y Felipe salgan.	I want Paco and Felipe to leave.
Quieren hacer el trabajo.	They want to do the work.
Quieren que ella haga el trabajo.	They want her to do the work.
Quieren volver mañana.	They want to return tomorrow.
Quieren que ella vuelva mañana.	They want her to return tomorrow.
Queremos decir algo.	We want to say something.
Queremos que Ana diga algo.	We want Ana to say something.
comprar---Dudo que ellos compren.	to buy--I doubt that they buy.
escuchar---Dudan que yo escuche.	to listen to--They doubt that I listen.
pensar---Dudamos que el animal piense.	to think--We doubt that the animal thinks.
venir---Siento que Fernando venga.	to come--I am sorry that Fernando is coming.
llegar---Ellos sienten que la familia llegue tarde.	to arrive--They are sorry that the family arrives late.
explicar---Sentimos que ellos no expliquen el problema.	to explain--We are sorry that they do not explain the problem.
ir---Es importante que Ud. vaya ahora mismo.	to go--It is important for you to go right now.
dar---Es posible que la niña me dé un regalo.	to give--It is possible that the girl will give me a gift.
ser---Es lástima que ellos no sean los padrinos.	to be--It is a shame that they are not the godparents.
saber---Es preciso que nosotros sepamos la respuesta.	to know--It is important that we know the answer.

EXERCISES COMPARING THE PRESENT AND PRETERITE VERBS (Chapters 7 and 10)

Hoy hablo---Ayer hablé	Today I speak---Yesterday I spoke (did speak)
Hoy converso---Ayer conversé	Today I converse---Yesterday I conversed
Hoy compro---Ayer compre	Today I buy---Yesterday I bought
Hoy llego---Ayer llegué	Today I arrive---Yesterday I arrived
Hoy pago---Ayer pagué	Today I pay---Yesterday I paid
Hoy explico---Ayer expliqué	Today I explain---Yesterday I explained
Hoy busco---Ayer busqué	Today I look---Yesterday I looked
Hoy comienzo---Ayer comencé	Today I begin---Yesterday I began
Hoy rezo---Ayer recé	Today I pray---Yesterday I prayed
Hoy recuerdo---Ayer recordé	Today I remember---Yesterday I remembered
Hoy me lavo---Ayer me lavé	Today I wash myself---Yesterday I washed myself
Hoy como---Ayer comí---Ayer comimos	Today I eat--Yesterday I ate--Yesterday we ate
Hoy aprendo---Ayer aprendí---Ayer aprendimos	Today I learn--Yesterday I learned--Yesterday we learned
Hoy salgo---Ayer salí---Ayer salimos	Today I leave--Yesterday I left--Yesterday we left
Hoy voy---Ayer fui---Ayer fuimos	Today I go--Yesterday I went--Yesterday we went
Hoy me pongo---Ayer me puse---Ayer nos pusimos	Today I put on--Yesterday I put on--Yesterday we put on
Hoy tengo---Ayer tuve---Ayer tuvimos	Today I have--Yesterday I had--Yesterday we had

Hoy hago---Ayer hice---Ayer hicimos | Today I do (make)--Yesterday I did--Yesterday we did

Hoy Ud. habla---Ayer Ud. habló---Ayer Ud. hablaron | Today you speak--Yesterday you spoke--Yesterday you (pl.) spoke
Hoy Ud. está---Ayer Ud. estuvo---Ayer Ud. estuvieron | Today you are--Yesterday you were--Yesterday you (pl.) were
Hoy Ud. da---Ayer Ud. dio---Ayer Uds. dieron | Today you give--Yesterday you gave--Yesterday you (pl.) gave
Hoy Ud. dice---Ayer Ud. dijo---Ayer Uds. dijeron | Today you say--Yesterday you (sing. and pl.) said
Hoy Ud. lee---Ayer Ud. leyó---Ayer Uds. leyeron | Today you read--Yesterday you (sing. and pl.)read
Hoy Ud. cree---Ayer Ud. creyó---Ayer Uds. creyeron | Today you believe--Yesterday you (sing. and pl.) believed
Hoy Ud. bebe---Ayer Ud. bebió---Ayer Uds. bebieron | Today you drink--Yesterday you (sing. and pl.)drank
Hoy Ud. predica---Ayer Ud. predicó--Ayer Uds. predicaron | Today you preach--Yesterday you (sing. and pl.) preached
Hoy Ud. ofrece---Ayer Ud. ofreció---Ayer Uds. ofrecieron | Today you offer--Yesterday you (sing. and pl.) offered
Hoy Ud. se lava---Ayer Ud. se lavó---Ayer Uds. se lavaron | Today you wash yourself--Yesterday you (sing. and pl.) washed
A Ud. le gusta---Ayer le gustó---Ayer a Uds. les gustó | Today you like it---Yesterday you (sing. and pl.) like it

EXERCISES WITH THE PRESENT PERFECT TENSE

hablar por teléfono---Yo.....he hablado por teléfono. | to speak on the phone--I...have spoken on the phone.
confesar---Este señor no.....ha confesado. | to confess---This man....has not confessed.
saber la verdad---Los discípulos.....han sabido la verdad. | to know the truth--The disciples...have known the truth.
ponerse el suéter---Yo.....me he puesto el suéter. | to put on a sweater--I.....have put on the sweater.
tocar la campana---Ud.....ha tocado la campana. | to ring the bell---You....have rung the bell. (*timbre = doorbell*)
visitar a los enfermos---Ellas.....han visitado a los enfermos. | to visit the sick---They....have visited the sick.
llamar por teléfono---Ese hombre....ha llamado por teléfono. | to call on the phone---That man.....has called on the phone.
tener hambre---Nosotros ....no hemos tenido hambre. | to be hungry---We.....haven't been hungry.
dormir la siesta---Los niños.....han dormido la siesta. | to take a nap---The children....have taken a nap.
no decir nada---La enfermera.....no ha dicho nada. | to not say anything---The nurse....has not said anything.

PRESENT PERFECT COMPARED WITH PLUPERFECT

(Yo) he trabajado---Había trabajado por horas. | I have worked---I had worked for hours.
Ellos han escuchado---Habían escuchado la homilía. | They have listened--They had listen to the homily.
Hemos leído---Habíamos leído el evangelio. | We have read---We had read the Gospel.
Él ha visto---Había visto los ángeles. | He has seen---He had seen the angels.
(Yo) he pensado---Había pensado en los feligreses. | I have thought---I had thought about the parishioners.
Uds. han vuelto---Uds. habían vuelto a la iglesia. | You (pl.) have returned---You had returned to church.
Ella ha comenzado---Había comenzado su carrera. | She has started---She had started her career.
(Yo) he ayudado---Había ayudado a los niños. | I have helped---I had helped the children.
Ellos se han lavado---Se habían lavado las manos. | They have washed---They had washed their hands.
Hemos escrito---Habíamos escrito las cartas. | We have written---We had written the letters.

Me ha gustado---Me había gustado la sorpresa.
A él le ha gustado---A él le había gustado mucho.
María ha dicho---María me había dicho algo.
Ellos han vivido---Ellos habían vivido en la ciudad.

I have liked---I had liked the surprise.
He has liked it---He had liked it a lot.
Mary has told---Mary had told me something.
They have lived---They had lived in the city.

EXERCISES WITH REFLEXIVE VERBS (Chapter 8)

Lavarse--Yo me lavo.
   Anita se lava el pelo.
   La enfermera se lavaba las manos.
   Ellos se lavaron antes de comer.
   Nos lavaremos más tarde.
sentarse--Yo me siento.
   La madre se sienta con su bebé.
   Ud. se sentó en la silla.
   Vamos a sentarnos porque estamos cansados.
ponerse--Yo me pongo el abrigo.
   En la primavera ella siempre se ponía un sombrero.
   Estaban poniéndose los zapatos.
   Quiero que ella se ponga el suéter.
   Póngase Ud. el sombrero. Póngaselo Ud.
   No se ponga Ud. el sombrero. No se lo ponga Ud.
casarse--Me caso con Gerardo.
   Quiero casarme con María Victoria.
   Ellos se casarán en la catedral.
   No es posible casarse sin los documentos necesarios.

to wash oneself--I wash myself
   Anita washes her hair.
   The nurse was washing her hands.
   They washed up before eating.
   We will wash up a little later.
to seat oneself--I will sit down.
   The mother sits with her baby.
   You sat down in the chair.
   We are going to sit down because we are tired.
to put on (clothing)--I put on a coat.
   In the spring she used to always put on a hat.
   They were putting on their shoes.
   I want her to put on her sweater.
   Put on you hat. Put it on.
   Don't put on you hat. Don't put it on.
to get married--I'm getting married to Gerardo. (Note the
   I want to maryy Maria Victoria.   preposition *con*)
   They will get married in the cathedral.
   It is possible to get married without the necessary documents.

EXERCISES WITH DIRECT OBJECT PRONOUNS

Compré muchos regalos---Los compré.
Vimos a muchos parientes---Los vimos.
Estamos estudiando el libro---Estamos estudiándolo.
Voy a ver la película francesa---Voy a verla./ La voy a ver.
Escribí las cartas anoche---Las escribí anoche.
Ellos quieren ver a los niños---Ellos quieren verlos.
Los jueves compro muchas flores---Los jueves las compro.

I bought many gifts---I bought them.
We saw many relatives---We saw them.
We are studying the book---We are studying it.
I am going to see the French film. I am going to see it. (2 ways)
I wrote the letters last night---I wrote them last night.
They want to see the children--They want to see them.
On Thursdays I buy lots of flowers--On Thursdays I buy them.